Confronting
Nonpromotability

How to Manage
a Stalled Career

EDWARD ROSEMAN

amacom
A Division of American Management Associations

Library of Congress Cataloging in Publication Data

Roseman, Edward.
    Confronting nonpromotability.

    Includes index.
    1. Promotions. I. Title. II. Title: Nonpromotability.
HF5549.5.P7R67   658.31'44   77-8013
ISBN 0-8144-5441-0

First Printing

Preface

The corporate elite are the "promotables." These upward bound men and women get special attention, tender loving care, and management grooming. They enjoy the status and rewards of having been chosen as heirs apparent to future titles. Most importantly, they have the personal satisfaction of knowing they're going someplace.

More numerous and far less satisfied are the "nonpromotables." They have been designated, officially or unofficially, as unworthy of consideration for upgrading. In other words, they will not be given the opportunity for promotion in the foreseeable future. Nor will they be lavished with attention, grooming, status, and rewards. The nonpromotables become depersonalized members of a growing army of second-class citizens. Management expects less from them and gives them less. As their years with the company pass by, they are expected to comply with an unspoken gentleman's agreement that condemns them to mediocrity:

Meet relatively easy-to-reach standards and don't complain about a diminishing organizational role. In return for your obedience, you keep your job and receive token rewards until you reach the upper limits of your salary range. By then, your accumulated pension benefits and age will lock you into an unsatisfying future.

No wonder the competition for promotion is so fierce. Everyone yearns for increasing rewards and unlimited promotional opportunities. And with the winners getting all, who wants to lose?

Yet, almost all become nonpromotable. It's just a matter of time. As you can see from the diagram on the next page, once you have been in a job long enough to master it, your boss assesses your promotability. If you get a favorable rating, you start moving up the career ladder as openings occur until you reach your top career step. Eventually, you too become nonpromotable.

After ten years of steady advancement, I was passed over for promotion. When I complained to my boss, she leveled with me. According to her, I was performing at the limit of my abilities, and my talents didn't match the corporation's future needs.

I don't know what bothered me more — the detached way in which she told me I was going nowhere, or the prospect of having to remain in the same job for the rest of my work career. Naturally, I disagreed with her. I argued and tried to convince her that she was wrong. But I had the uncomfortable feeling that she was right. My immediate reaction was to quit, but I had heavy personal responsibilities, and it had taken me ten years to earn my current place in the company. Besides, I wasn't confident I could start out at the same level in another company.

In subsequent months, my relationship with my boss was strained. But I began to adjust to reality and decided to hang on to my present job. Maybe I wouldn't feel about the job as I had in the past, but I could learn to live with the situation.

Variations on this theme are repeated daily in every company. People learn that their careers will not be advanced at some point, but it may take considerable time before they are able to stop fighting it.

Dead-ended people may escape temporarily to other companies, where they resume their upward mobility until the next career impasse. However, after protest, they finally accept the sentence of nonpromotability. When that happens, their work commitment, energy level, and productivity tend to decline.

Thus, nonpromotability has major impact not only on the individual, but on managers who supervise nonpromotables as well as the corporations which accumulate a growing number of them each year.

The Certainty of Nonpromotability

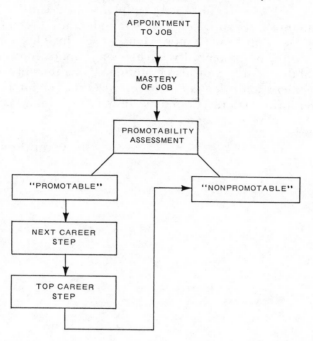

Because of the severe impact of nonpromotability and the magnitude of this problem, I feel compelled to focus attention on it. Managers and corporations can help the nonpromotables look forward to the future, develop themselves, and experience a sense of fulfillment in their work. It is possible for them to offset dwindling financial rewards and lack of advancement with equally satisfying psychological rewards. Stale people and stale jobs can be revitalized, and a motivating work environment for the nonpromotable can be created.

There's more than a humanitarian incentive for helping the nonpromotable. Since most people fall into that category eventually, failure to be concerned with their full utilization and development can have substantial effects on profit. Therefore, to protect their competence and productivity makes good business sense. The nonpromotable deserves as much attention and management interest as the promotable.

I am indebted to the administration of the Pharmaceutical/ Chemical MBA Program at Fairleigh Dickinson University for encouraging and supporting me as founder and director of its Career Development Center. Many of my insights into the subject of nonpromotability have been gained from experiences at the Center. I am also grateful to the editors of *Product Management* and *Medical Laboratory Observer* for permission to reprint material from those of my articles that have appeared in these magazines.

EDWARD ROSEMAN

Contents

PART ONE
Concerns of the Manager

1   Understanding the Process of Becoming Nonpromotable   3
     Worksheet 1   Early Warning System for Nonpromotability / 18

2   Counseling Nonpromotables   23
     Worksheet 2   The Counseling Interview / 32
     Worksheet 3   Counseling Self-Evaluation Ratings / 37

3   Development — An Investment or a Waste?   42
     Worksheet 4   The Developmental Interview / 57

4   Revitalizing Stale People and Stale Jobs   61

5   Creating a Motivating Job Environment   79
     Worksheet 5   Subordinate–Superior Relationship / 82

6   The Helping Appraisal   98

7   Redirecting Aging Careers   119

8   Untangling Destructive Mismatches   130
     Worksheet 6   Alternatives to Termination / 138
     Worksheet 7   When to Salvage the Failing Subordinate / 141

PART TWO
Concerns of the Individual

9   Nonpromotable by Whose Yardstick?   149
       Worksheet 8   Rating Your Boss / 151
       Worksheet 9   Challenging the Justness of Nonpromotability/ 164

10   Changing Jobs for Something Better or Escaping?   168
       Worksheet 10   Peer Comparison Ratings / 169
       Worksheet 11   Comparison of Current and New Jobs / 175

11   Becoming a "Lifer"   185

12   Adapting Successfully to Nonpromotability   202
       Worksheet 12   Choosing *Right* Alternatives / 205
       Worksheet 13   Daily Work Balance Sheet / 213

13   Life and Career Planning   220
       Worksheet 14   Calculating the Probability of Career Change / 221
       Worksheet 15   Life and Career Planning / 226

14   A Final Message   239

       Index   241

PART ONE

Concerns
of the Manager

CHAPTER ONE

Understanding the Process of Becoming Nonpromotable

Nonpromotability sneaks up on most people. It rarely happens in exactly the same way to different individuals. Yet, although the patterns are varied and the precipitating events sometimes almost undetectable, the man or woman prepared for it and alert to the symptoms can make an early diagnosis. This book will help you understand the inevitable process of becoming nonpromotable by examining it, by classifying its forms, and by picking out its significant warning signs.

The insidiousness of nonpromotability has been protected by the fact that it has never been a subject for open discussion. Because there is a stigma attached to being nonpromotable, bosses don't want to talk to subordinates about it and subordinates don't want to listen to any suggestions that it may be happening to them. It therefore attacks victims who had hoped to escape it by ignoring it.

Nonpromotability can't be escaped, but it can often be delayed, and its impact can always be softened. By gaining an insight into the point at which nonpromotability is most likely to occur, as well as how and why it happens, people are able to face what is threatening them. Surprise is prevented by full exposure to the problem, which then enables one to create stronger defensive action. It also allows for more favorable terms of surrender.

ONSET, DEVELOPMENT, and FIXATION

The process of nonpromotability has three distinct phases —
onset, development, and fixation. However, the duration of
each phase and the number of jobs a person may hold within
each phase vary greatly. A common pattern is one in which the
onset stage occurs within the first five years of a career, usually
on the second job. During the onset stage, you come to recognize your place within the pecking order. You begin to ask
yourself certain questions to compare yourself with the other
people who are competing for advancement:

Am I as smart as they?
Do I work harder?
Do my boss and peers like me any better?
Am I accomplishing more?
Am I politically adept at maneuvering for advantages?
What is the relative quality and quantity of my work in com-
parison with that of others?

When the answers indicate that the competition has an
upper hand, you have entered the development stage of
nonpromotability. As a career matures, the possibility that one
will not advance usually develops rapidly during years five to
ten. In this stage, job switching is common, with people on the
average holding from two to four different jobs. The same
questions you ask yourself during the onset stage apply during
the development stage, but verification of answers by other
people whose opinions you value adds to the significance of
the answers. Perhaps you have had unfavorable or less-than-
favorable annual appraisals, or increases in salary come less
frequently than you think they should or than those received
by others. A disparity between your pay and that of others
with comparable work experience has become painfully apparent, and differences in the rate of advancement have become readily observable. The feelings of such a person are
vividly described by an accountant employed by a major
auditing firm:

It's not fair. I've been a CPA since I was twenty-three years old. I
was one of the youngest CPAs in the state. Now, eight years later,
many of the guys I graduated with and who received their CPAs after

I did are already partners in public accounting firms. And, by the way they live with the big cars, fancy houses, and elaborate vacations, I know they're making a hell of a lot more money than I am. In the last eight years I worked for three different companies. Each time I thought the size of the company, the boss I was working for, or the number of opportunities was holding me back. So I left for greener pastures. The company I'm with now is one of the biggest and most respected companies in the business. I work for a decent boss, whom I believe I get along with, and there are plenty of openings. For some reason, I'm just not the one who is considered for those openings. Something's definitely wrong!

The fixation stage of the nonpromotability process is usually time-related; on the average it occurs after at least the third job. By the time this stage is reached everyone, including those who try to ignore reality, has become aware that his or her future aspirations probably will never be attained. Men and women whose careers are in the fixation stage are in their thirties, forties, fifties, and the final preretirement years. Their energy has waned and their competitiveness and aggressiveness have probably been replaced by hostility and bitterness or just plain indifference. Questions that help to confirm the fact that you have passed into the fixation stage are:

Is my next career step certain?
Have I accumulated detractors during the past years?
Are there any blemishes on my performance record?
Do I work as hard now as I used to?
Do I enjoy my job as much as I did in past years?
Has my rate of learning and development decreased?
Am I as concerned about the future as I have been in the past?
Do others who are important to my career act as if they are still considering me for future opportunities?

Asking yourself such blunt questions may be upsetting, because the answers tend to destroy self-esteem. The prospect of being fixed in the same job, or, worse yet, in jobs of lesser importance, is both frightening and depressing. In fact, the realization that one is not going any further in one's career often brings men and women battling deep, emotional problems to the psychiatrist's couch.

FIGURE 1
Process of nonpromotability.

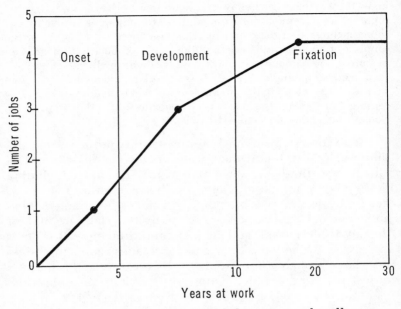

The three stages of nonpromotability are graphically represented in Figure 1.

Now let's take a close look at the complexities of nonpromotability by examining some typical case histories. A matrix has
been designed to assist in analyzing the nonpromotability
process by relating factors of time, awareness, and acceptance
to the three stages of the process. We will use these param-
eters to help analyze the career stories of three fictitious
people.

	Time	Awareness	Acceptance
Onset			
Development			
Fixation			

Case One

Mike is a tall, good-looking, well-dressed salesman in his
early thirties. He's married and has five children. His dad is a

factory worker, and all his relatives have a blue-collar background. Mike had an effortless C average in high school and probably would never have gone to college had he not received a football scholarship. In college he was an indifferent, if adequate, student. He received a degree in business administration with a major in marketing.

Mike's work history has been distinguished by multiple job changes — four jobs in nine years — with ups and downs in performance. One of his bosses explained his erratic performance by saying, "Mike's a money player. When he needs money, he works like a demon. When financial pressures ease, he tends to coast. He doesn't want money just for the sake of earning money; he works for what money can buy." He has changed jobs on several occasions to increase his salary earnings. Although he claims he's interested in advancement, he has done little but talk about it. He rarely reads, has not taken any postgraduate courses, and doesn't attend any workshops or participate in trade organizations.

Outside the job, Mike has many interests as well as problems. As a former athlete, he is still interested in participative sports. He's a star in a softball league, plays tennis all year 'round, and likes to bowl. When he's not actively involved with sports, he's attending games or watching them on television. His preoccupation with sports interferes with his relationship with his wife. And in the course of years, his marriage has become increasingly strained, particularly because he's a heavy drinker and spender.

Mike took a standard personality test, The Edwards Personal Preference Schedule developed in 1954 by Dr. Allen L. Edwards of the University of Washington. The results of Mike's test showed the following characteristics: He likes to talk about himself and be the center of attention; he finds it difficult to finish assignments, to work without distraction; he has a strong need to have as many friends as possible and to do things with friends rather than alone; he has little inclination to be self-analytical and is relatively insensitive to the feelings and motives of others; on the other hand, he wants others to be kindly and sympathetic to him. Finally, he likes to do new and different things and to meet new people.

Mike's completed matrix looks like this:

	Time	Awareness	Acceptance
Onset	early	unaware	no
Development	early	unaware	no
Fixation	early	unaware	no

The onset of Mike's nonpromotability occurred early in his career. In fact, he progressed through all three stages of the process rapidly, and after four jobs in nine years, he is stuck in the fixation stage of nonpromotability.

Despite this rapid deterioration, Mike is unaware of what has been happening to him. If questioned, he still believes, "Someday I'm going to make it big. Other people are going to realize that I've got what it takes to be the sales manager of a company. I'm wasted as a salesman."

Naturally, because he's unaware that he has entered the fixation stage of nonpromotability, he is not facing an acceptance problem. There's no adjustment for him to make because he doesn't acknowledge that he has a problem. And as he's still in his early thirties, his fantasies persist. As he grows older, though, it's unlikely that his fantasies will survive.

Case Two

Paul is a distinguished man in his fifties. He looks and acts like what he is, a successful executive in a large advertising agency. The product of a socially prominent family, he had an Ivy League education and he earned bachelor's and master's degrees in business with distinction. In the Navy he was an officer with an impressive record of accomplishments.

In his 25-year work career, he has held five jobs in which he advanced rapidly both in title and salary. His high intelligence, energy level, and capacity for hard work have served him well.

In the past, he left jobs to accelerate his career. Invariably, he was given, and refused, attractive counteroffers from past employers. Although he was ambitious to the point where he has been accused of being "cold and ruthless," his performance has always been highly respected. He has worked hard to hone his skills by participating actively in self-development programs. Moreover, he has kept at jobs until they were finished. But he had no need to form strong personal attachments, seldom helped friends when they were in trouble, and enjoyed changes in daily routine and experimenting with new things.

In contrast, his life outside the job has been a mess. He has been divorced twice, and his relationship with his only child has been poor. In addition, the toll of "all work and no play" has had him in psychoanalysis for many years and has plagued him with a variety of psychosomatic disorders. His personality test scores show that he has strong drives toward achievement, autonomy, dominance, and aggression.

Paul's matrix is quite different from Mike's. He entered the three stages of nonpromotability late in his career, and the duration of each stage was very short. In fact, the total process has occurred within a period of less than five years.

	Time	Awareness	Acceptance
Onset	late	unaware	no
Development	late	unaware	no
Fixation	late	aware	no

Because the process developed so rapidly, he was unaware of what was happening until he was in the fixation stage.

He is a very sensitive man who continually analyzes the motives, feelings, and behavior of himself and others; yet despite the benefit of professional counsel, he refuses to realize that he is no longer promotable. He laments the fact that the headhunters no longer call him and that informal probes directed at higher-level jobs in other companies have been rebuffed. Within his own organization there are a limited number of openings available to him, and although he is not being considered for top-level jobs, he still hopes for advancement.

Case Three

Arnie is a mixed breed—half blue collar and half white collar—who at forty is content with life and proud of his accomplishments. He has a devoted wife, two lovely children, a modest but comfortable home, and savings in the bank.

Although hindered by minimal education (he had enlisted

in the Army on graduation from high school and hadn't continued his education thereafter), he has a solid record of accomplishments. In the Army, he was a noncommissioned officer; he learned enough about electronic equipment to earn himself a job as a technician in private industry.

His entire work history has been with a single company. After ten years of consistent performance, he became a group supervisor and has held that job for the past five years. In that capacity he has earned the respect and friendship of both his peers and his superiors. He's relatively happy in his job, but he would like to be promoted. However, evidently he's not unhappy enough to take some positive action, such as participating in self-development activities or even changing jobs to go to another company where there might be greater opportunities.

Most of his outside activities involve his family and friends. The only exception is that he is active in church-related activities.

Arnie's personality test shows that he's high in conformity and very conventional. He's happy to get suggestions from others and to follow instructions. He has strong loyalty to friends. He likes to participate in friendly groups and wants to be helpful to others. He's low in aggression and dominance, and he tends to feel timid in the presence of superiors and inferior in general. He doesn't analyze his own motives and feelings or those of others. Finally, he's very resistant to change.

Matrix analysis of Arnie's career shows that the onset stage of nonpromotability began early, but its process was interrupted by an unexpected promotion. He reentered the onset stage in the new job after a short time, and it is now apparent that this job is probably a dead end. The development and fixation stages have progressed rapidly.

	Time	Awareness	Acceptance
Onset	early	unaware	yes
Development	early	aware	yes
Fixation	early	aware	yes

During the onset stage he had been basically unaware that his prospects for promotion were poor, but after the long-delayed promotion, he probably entertains dim hopes for another one. Since his drive for promotion is low and he's content with his work and home life, Arnie accepts slow advancement calmly.

The foregoing analysis has emphasized the dimensions of time, awareness, and acceptance. Additional factors are age; family responsibilities and relationships; economic background; basic intelligence; education; work history, particularly reasons for quitting jobs, accomplishments. relationships with peers and superiors, participation in self-development activities; off-the-job interests and problems; and personality factors.

THE WHYS and WHEREFORES

Before we integrate these variables into an early warning system for nonpromotability, other questions are worthwhile exploring. Is nonadvancement voluntary or involuntary? Is it temporary or permanent? Is it real or perceived? Is it related to situational factors or to basic factors, such as ability, motivation, and effectiveness? Is nonpromotability the result of embarking on the wrong career path, of becoming too specialized or not specialized enough? What part does politics play? How do fear, resistance to change, and lack of introspection interfere with promotability? What is the impact of past performance, particularly past mistakes?

Voluntary vs. Involuntary

Participants in career-planning workshops were forced to challenge their attitudes about promotion by responding to the following questions. How important is promotion to you? If it meant relocation, dramatic increase in work hours and time away from home, or other major sacrifices, under what conditions would you accept promotion (assuming the promotion was a desirable one and represented a substantial increase in status, responsibility, and compensation)?

Would you accept the promotion unconditionally, regardless of the sacrifices that would have to be made?

Would you expect sacrifices to be specifically defined, and

would you not accept promotion if your current way of life were affected strongly?

Are you willing to make only minor changes in your current way of life in order to accept promotion?

Only a small percentage were willing to accept promotions unconditionally. Most had a wide range of opinion as to what kinds of sacrifices they were willing to make and to what degree they would change their way of life. They withdrew from competition for promotion either consciously or unconsciously when potential sacrifices were viewed as beyond acceptable limits.

Of course, there are many people who are willing to make the necessary sacrifices and who yearn for promotion. But either they don't have the opportunity, or they are less attractive candidates than are their competitors. For them, promotion is not voluntarily refused. No choice is involved.

Temporary vs. Permanent

Individuals may become nonpromotable in the near future, in the distant future, or forever. For someone who has a strong desire for a quick promotion, even temporary nonpromotability is unbearable. Others may deliberately withdraw from consideration for promotion because of temporary personal problems, such as illness in the family, school considerations, community commitments, and so forth. Generally, the further into the future a possible promotion is, the more likely one is to think of himself or herself as nonpromotable and therefore succumb to the decline in energy levels and productivity associated with nonpromotability: "What's the sense in breaking my back when I can't see any advancement in the future? My boss is just a few years older than I am, and he's not going anyplace in a hurry."

Real vs. Perceived

When someone thinks he or she has reached a dead end, it's as real as if it were a fact. These people may search prematurely for new jobs or turn off on their present jobs. People who have low self-esteem are most likely to make unfavorable comparisons between themselves and their immediate competitors. This often results in a self-fulfilling prophecy—by convincing themselves that they're not as good as others, they perform below their capabilities, making their competitors look better.

No-Win Situations

"Wrong time, wrong place, wrong cast of characters" can have a profound effect on promotability. Generally, the person who works for a company with declining sales has fewer promotional opportunities than does someone in a company that is growing rapidly. Or someone who gets stuck in a work unit that has major problems may find that his reputation or image has been dirtied by a mess for which he has no responsibility. It's a no-win situation in which no matter how hard that person tries, the results will be unfavorable. And pity the poor person who works for an incompetent supervisor or one who just doesn't like him. He'll rot in the job.

Basic Nonpromotability

Whereas situational factors are powerful forces, they can still be overcome. At least there is hope for those who suffer from situational nonpromotability. But there is no hope for those who are basically nonpromotable. These are the unfortunates who just don't have sufficient intelligence and ability to perform at a higher-level job. Their problem is described accurately by the personnel manager of a major company:

They just can't hack it. Some things—creativity, judgment, courage, energy, confidence, analytical ability, foresight, resourcefulness, drive—you either have or you don't. Training is pitifully inadequate at correcting major deficiencies. It's as hopeless as marrying someone you hope to remake.

Wrong Career Paths—Too Specialized or Not Specialized Enough?

"How can I give a nonscientist the responsibility of a manager of a research and development group?" a top manager complained in a roundtable discussion.

"How can I expect a staff lawyer to move up into a line management slot?" asked another top manager.

In a roundtable discussion on the subject of nonpromotability, both managers had presented cases that involved top performers who had become dead-ended. In one case a production manager had applied for an opening as administrative director of the R&D labs. He was told he wasn't qualified for the job because he lacked specialized experience. The other case involved a valuable member of the legal staff who aspired to a line management role and was told he was too specialized to perform as a generalist. Certainly the objections raised were legitimate. On the other hand, some people are automatically excluded unjustifiably from consideration for promotion because of the issue of specialization.

Starting on the wrong career path as a result of past education and work experience may doom the advancement of many individuals. This is often what happens to specialists such as chemists who have earned a master's degree before entering the industry, and who thereafter had no opportunity to earn a doctorate. Their forward progress in their specialty is blocked by lack of an advanced degree. Similarly, someone who has had a succession of marketing research positions will probably find it difficult to gain serious consideration for upward mobility outside the specialty in which he or she has had experience. Midcareer changes are possible but not in many work environments.

Politics — How Much or How Little?

The person who minds his own business and concentrates on his work tasks is surprised and bitter to learn that his work style has cost him advancement. For example, listen to the deep frustration and anger of an assistant purchasing agent in a large manufacturing organization who had it happen to him:

> While I worked fifty to sixty hours each week handling a monstrous work load, some of the other assistant purchasing agents took two-hour lunches and spent half the day office-hopping and scoring political points with the brass. I convinced myself that politicking could not take the place of hard work. Eventually, my performance would speak louder than their backslapping and personal campaigning. But was I wrong! One of the politicos with less than half my time on the job and less training and experience ended up as my boss. I had to fight to contain myself when he told me he was sure that we would work well together since he knew how conscientious and efficient I was. Of course he was delighted — he was now in control of a work

horse who could perform a hell of a lot better than he could. That's what I call a typical case of organizational justice.

Those who work the hardest, put in the longest hours, and try the most are not necessarily guranteeing their promotability. Fitting into an environment and doing what has to be done are sometimes even more important than performance. This is especially true for someone who is part of a group in which individual performance is difficult to appraise.

However, those who compromise their level of performance because they're too busy politicking may destroy their chances for promotion. Company politicos tend to accumulate detractors as well as supporters. If these detractors are in high places, or if one of them is the immediate superior, an impenetrable wall may be constructed between an individual and his or her next career step. Furthermore, politicos aligned with those currently in power may be forced to watch helplessly as their allies and all those associated with them lose control.

Here's a sad tale of lost promotability, told by a company controller who found himself at the losing end of a political battle:

I thought my future was assured. The executive vice president in charge of finance was my mentor, and he was one of the closest advisers of the president. My loyalty to them was unshakable. Things were going great for the company and for me, but a personality clash between the chairman of the board and the president cost him his job. The executive vice president in charge of finance, the confidant of the president, went next. And, of course, my strong association with what had become the enemy camp made my own position untenable. My job was downgraded and my power disappeared. I quit and then spent nearly eight months and all my savings searching for a new job. Ironically, I felt lucky when I finally found a job at a lower level and salary then I had in my previous company.

Fear and Other Emotions

In his book *What Are You Afraid Of?* John T. Wood describes the relationship of fear to anger, guilt, dependency, insecurity, and frustration.* A business environment is fertile

---

*John T. Wood, *What Are You Afraid Of? A Guide to Dealing With Your Fears* (Englewood Cliffs, N.J.: Prentice-Hall, 1976), pp. 46–55.

ground for fear—fear of failure, fear of punishment, fear of rejection. These anxieties in turn feed other negative emotions, which rob people of their self-confidence and inhibit their actions. It's a vicious cycle. The more an individual fears that he may fail and evoke disapproval and punishment, the more threatened he becomes. The more threatened he is, the more cautious and unwilling he is to act, which makes him dependent and insecure. This makes him feel angry with himself and others, guilty for not taking action, and frustrated because his lack of action hurts his performance and his chances for advancement. Those who allow fear to become their master are also its victims:

I enjoyed my job up to the time my self-esteem and job status became entangled. I thrived in the status and power of my position. I stopped focusing on upward mobility because I was worried about keeping what I had already gained. Suppose I couldn't handle the next job upward and screwed up everything I had worked so hard for? Maybe I was lucky for coming as far as I had. Would the Peter Principle catch up with me? I couldn't look upward as long as I was looking downward.

Past Performance and Past Mistakes

Performance appraisal is subject to overrating and underrating. Those who perform certain tasks outstandingly are generally considered to be outstanding; those who perform some things poorly, particularly if they have made noteworthy mistakes, are rated poorly. Like an artist who draws caricatures, the appraiser tends to exaggerate prominent differences.

The fact that one person—an immediate supervisor—generally has sole responsibility for an appraisal contributes to distortion in performance appraisals. The immediate superior reports things as seen through his or her eyes and incorporates personal biases, likes, and dislikes. Because objective data are filtered through a subjective screen, you may accumulate undeserved marks, both good and bad. Unfortunately, the bad marks often attract more attention than the good marks. And a track record soiled by too many bad marks puts you out of contention for promotional openings. And so although performance has a profound effect on one's promotability, it certainly isn't an absolute. There is no real "fair balance.

AN EARLY WARNING SYSTEM

If you or one of your subordinates are concerned about future promotability, the nonpromotability early warning system in Worksheet 1 will be a valuable aid. Each dimension of nonpromotability is challenged and rated as positive, negative, or neutral. If you feel very positive about a specific item, a +3 is recorded in the space next to the item. Lesser degrees of positiveness are recorded as +2 or +1 ratings. Similarly, if you feel very negative about an item, record a −3 rating. For lesser feelings of negativism, rate −2 or −1. If you are neither negative nor positive about an item, or if you are uncertain, record a neutral score of 0.

The total score has no absolute significance. Its meaning is significant only in relation to scores accumulated over a period of time and to self-ratings compared with ratings made by others you trust. In addition, the size of the negative score compared with that of the positive score is important. In workshops that use the early warning system, it was found that people whose negative score was higher than their positive score were invariably experiencing problems with advancement. In fact, those with negative scores above 40 were already in the development stage of nonpromotability. Particularly sensitive indicators were the dimensions of time, competitive differences, and work history.

The following explanation of the challenges listed in column 2 of the worksheet will help you to use the system properly.

Time. How does your age compare with that of other people with the same job title in your own company and in other companies? If you're younger, record a positive score. If you're older, record a negative score. If you're about the same age, record a neutral score. How long have you been in the same job in comparison with others in similar jobs? How do you feel about the length of time you have been in that job? As in the first item, record your degree of positive or negative feelings, using a −3 to +3 scale.

WORKSHEET 1
Early warning system for nonpromotability.

+3 *Very positive*	−3 *Very negative*	0 *Neutral*
+2 *Positive*	−2 *Negative*	
+1 *Somewhat positive*	−1 *Somewhat negative*	

DIMENSIONS	*CHALLENGE*	+	−	0
Time	Age related to title?			
	Time in same job?			
Acceptance	Submissive?			
	Realistic?			
Awareness	Self-questioning?			
	Perceptive?			
Family	Relationships?			
	Responsibilities?			
Competitive differences	Intelligence?			
	Personality traits?			
	Self-confidence and self-esteem?			
	Abilities?			
	Drive and aspirations?			
	Attitudes?			
Education	Number of degrees?			
	Technical?			
Work history	Job changes?			
	Reasons for changing jobs?			
	Accomplishments and performance?			
Interpersonal relationships	Important others?			
	Peers?			
Development	Self?			
	By others?			
Opportunity	Short-term?			
	Foreseeable future?			
Stability	Financial?			
	Adaptability?			
	Self-discipline?			
	Total			

Acceptance. Do you accept your rate of advancement passively, or do you question it regularly? If you accept it passively, record a negative score. If you question it regularly, record a positive score. How realistic are your feelings about your rate of advancement? If you tend to strive for attainable goals, record a positive score. If you tend to wish for virtually unattainable goals, score negatively.

Awareness. Do you analyze your own motives, feelings, and behavior and observe them in others? If you do, score positively. If you're relatively unaware of yourself and others, score negatively. In your analysis of self and others, how perceptive are you? If you're usually on target, score positively. If you're often mistaken, score negatively.

Family. How are your intimate relationships? Do you have a happy home? Are there any problems with your family relationships that might interfere with your job? If your family is a source of strength, score positively. If it presents problems, score negatively. What kinds of responsibilities do you have? Is there any reason why you can't relocate, such as sick parents? If family responsibilities do not block your forward progress, score positively. If they do, score negatively.

Competitive Differences. How do you compare with others in terms of intelligence? Are you smarter? Not as smart? What about your personality traits, especially your needs for achievement, autonomy, and dominance? How resistant are you to change? What is your need for approval from friends and superiors? To what degree are you influenced by the need to belong to the peer group? How strong is your ability to keep at a job until it is finished? In other words, does your personality work for you or against you? If it works for you, score positively. If it works against you, score negatively.

How much self-confidence and self-esteem do you have? Do you do things because you believe in them or because you are trying to please others? If you are self-confident and have a good opinion of yourself, score positively. If not, negatively. How do you compare with your peers in managerial ability? Technical ability? What's required for your next career step, and how do your abilities match those requirements? If they match well, score positively. If not, score negatively. How strong are your drives and aspirations? Do you want to advance? How hard are you willing to work for advancement? What sacrifices are you willing to make? If you feel you will work harder than your competitors for job openings and are willing to pay the price for advancement, score positively. If not, negatively. How do your attitudes, particularly toward change, responsibility, and failure, help or hinder your progress? If you accept change, face the unknown with courage, are resilient, then score positively. If the opposite, score negatively.

Education. Do you have a college degree? Were your studies pertinent to your current job? Do you have advanced degrees? Will advanced degrees help you with a future job? How much technical training have you had? If your educational background matches your future job needs, score positively.

Work History. How many job changes have you made in your career? If you have not made any job changes, or have had fewer job changes than most of your colleagues, is it because you are afraid to make a change in order to advance yourself? If you've made a great many job changes, considerably more than your colleagues, did each contribute to your advancement? Too few or too many job changes can both be negatives, depending on circumstances. Of particular importance is whether you had valid reasons for making the moves. In each of your jobs, what performance ratings did you receive? Did you have outstanding accomplishments? If you were rated well and had outstanding accomplishments, score positively.

Interpersonal Relationships. How do you get along with others, particularly with important people, such as your boss or those who are in a position to affect your job advancement? How do you get along with peers? Although peers do not have direct bearing on your advancement, their feelings about you are indirectly reflected upward, thereby affecting the attitudes of those in important positions. If you get along well with others, score positively.

Development. Has your personal growth progressed at a faster rate than that of your competitors? Have you taken the initiative in your personal growth, attending postgraduate education courses, reading, participating in self-improvement projects? To what extent have others assisted you with your personal development? Do you have a mentor who has served as a model in giving you helpful counseling? If you have an active self-development program and are being carefully groomed by others, score positively.

Opportunity. Are there many job openings within your present company? Is the rate of growth of the company rapid, creating new promotional opportunities? Do you expect to reach your next career step in less than two years? If you don't expect short-term advancement, do you expect it in the foreseeable future, say in three to five years?

Stability. How well do you manage your financial situation? Do you have strong financial needs? Although the pressure for more money can sometimes be a spurt to advancement, it also forces you to rush your career and make wrong job decisions. If you have a reasonable desire for financial advancement but are not pressured by financial considerations, score positively. How adaptable are you? If you reach what appears to be a career impasse, can you change direction? Are you resilient enough to bounce back from failure? If you are adaptable, score positively. Finally, how much self-discipline do you have? Are you likely to cop out when the going gets rough? Will you be able to make an extra effort when necessary, and can you do so for sustained periods of time? If you have demonstrated self-discipline in the past, it's likely that it will serve you well in the future.

THE PAYOFF

Nonpromotability has been presented as a complex, multi-dimensional, dynamic process. It sneaks up on people because they are not alert to its warning signs and they don't detect the subtle but distinct stages of onset, development, and fixation. The payoff for better understanding of the process is threefold:

1. Understanding leads to more intelligent challenge of the justness and finality of nonpromotability; it protects you and the company from making premature judgments.
2. Understanding helps in planning realistic career paths.

3. Understanding helps soften the impact of nonpromotability, as early detection allows time both to prepare for it
   and accept it gracefully.

An effort to understand the process of nonpromotability requires continual study throughout your career. This chapter is
only a beginning — a step forward — in exploring a subject that
should be of vital concern to all working people. If you're interested in promotability, you should be equally interested in
its counterpart — nonpromotability.

CHAPTER TWO

Counseling Nonpromotables

Every daily face-to-face encounter with subordinates involves counseling to some extent. You give advice, opinions, instruction in an effort to direct the judgment or conduct of your subordinates. When properly given, counseling provides genuine help in recognizing and choosing a better way of behaving. However, because it is often mishandled, not only does it fail to accomplish its intended purpose, it even works against it.

Counseling someone who has reached an impasse in his or her career presents some very special considerations. Because the nonpromotable has been in a particular job for some time, he's likely to feel he has mastered it. This can make him resistant to change and overly sensitive to criticism.

Since a natural reaction to nonpromotability is resentment combined with varying degrees of nonacceptance, the superior–subordinate relationship may become strained. Furthermore, traditional motivational appeals aren't applicable for men and women on the down side of their careers. When their performance is slipping, you can't threaten, "This will hurt your chances of getting promoted," or, "If you want a decent raise in salary, you'd better shape up." You have to find different means to overcome dissatisfaction with their jobs, the company, and themselves. Finally, because the nonpromotable may think of himself as a "reject," his self-esteem is fragile. He'll employ a wide array of defense mechanisms to protect himself during the counseling interview.

Differences in dealing with nonpromotability are dramatized in the following vignettes.

Jane has been with the same company for fifteen years and in her current job for nearly 10 years. In a counseling interview with her boss, the discussion came to an impasse when she said, "Are you trying to tell me that after ten years I don't know what I'm doing? You're questioning things I've been doing the same way for years." By suggesting slight modifications in her work habits, Jane's boss had unknowingly attacked her personal competence and past accomplishments. She strenuously resisted any changes and magnified the mild criticism in her mind.

Counseling interviews with Steve were stormy. He resented having been passed over for promotion. Cognitively, he understood his personal failings, but "in his gut" he couldn't accept them. In counseling interviews he would repeatedly play the same broken record: "I'm sorry that you find fault with my performance, but it's hard for me to keep my mind on my job when I feel it's a blind alley. Even though we've discussed some of my personal shortcomings, I know I would do well at a higher-level job." He would only half-listen to suggestions on how to improve his current performance because he was still dreaming about "getting ahead."

As with many other nonpromotables, Sam's productivity and job satisfaction have been waning. In the past, his strong drive for money and power motivated him to work hard. Now, frozen in the same job for several years, he complains during counseling interviews: "With the cost of living rising faster than my salary and people with far less time with the company jumping over me into plush jobs, how can you expect me to perform as I used to? I'll give you a day's work for a day's pay. It's not fair for you to ask more of me." Considering his present circumstances, he feels he's performing adequately.

Thus, the manager responsible for counseling nonpromotables is faced with extraordinary problems. He has to help resistant, and often resentful, subordinates make positive behavior changes. Somehow, without being able to use money or advancement as motivators, he has to break through indifference, dissatisfaction, and defensiveness. And he must accomplish this without further injuring already fragile self-esteem. Counseling should only be undertaken when timing and conditions are right, and only after considerable planning.

FORMAL COUNSELING

One reason for ineffective counseling is that it is often spontaneous and unplanned. Your subordinate may initiate an on-the-spot request for help for which you are unprepared to give proper advice. He may ask for instructions in how to do something, solve a problem, or evaluate his performance. If you respond immediately with advice and solutions, you run a high risk of not really being helpful. You need time to learn the full meaning of the request for help or to gather sufficient facts.

Not all spontaneous, unplanned counseling is initiated by subordinates. Frequently, you may put yourself into an unwanted advice- or opinion-giving situation, which leads to impromptu counseling:

Subordinate: I've been having trouble with this new report.
Manager: Here, let me show you how to do it.

or

Manager: You're not doing that right. That's not the way I do it.

Formal, planned counseling can be far more effective than the impromptu variety because its purpose is better defined. You have an opportunity to prepare for the counseling interview. You have time to select the right setting and define your objectives.

The difference between spontaneous, unplanned counseling and formal, planned counseling is aptly described by a participant in a workshop I conducted:

Some managers have the gift of great insight and quick thinking and can give on-the-spot counseling of high quality. But most of us need time to think before we talk. I personally am very stingy with the counseling I give. That's because I don't want it to backfire. I make sure I understand the problem, have all the facts, and most importantly, don't give any advice until my subordinate really wants it and is ready to receive it.

Formal Counseling Opportunities

There are five types of formal counseling opportunities. The average manager should schedule these meetings on a regular basis.

1. *Instructional Counseling.* This may take the form of instruction in new skills or improvement of old skills. You assume the role of a teacher when you explain what to do and how to do it. To be successful, your subordinate must want to learn and must recognize you as someone who can teach him. Also, in counseling the nonpromotable, you should recognize that he must "unlearn" certain things before he undertakes new learning.

2. *Evaluative Counseling.* This is also called appraisal counseling. Many companies require an annual appraisal of all employees. Such appraisals are frequently perfunctory. Yet everybody wants to know, and expects to be told, what their managers think of their performance. The annual appraisal rarely serves this purpose as it is too general in nature, covers too long a period of time, and is rarely balanced (it is either highly critical or highly complimentary).

> "You're doing a great job. You're hard-working, energetic, thorough . . . "

or

> "I haven't been pleased with your performance. Your productivity is low, you're careless, you don't seem to get along well with other people in the department . . . "

You may feel it's a waste of time to appraise employees who have worked for you for some time. Over the years, you've told them how you feel about their performance deficiencies. Why reopen old wounds? But people who remain in the same position feel otherwise. They assume that you're uninterested in them and have brushed them off during the appraisal interview.

3. *Disciplinary Counseling.* This particularly unpleasant type of counseling is scheduled with reluctance. Uncomfort-

able with confrontation, you may beat around the bush in conducting this kind of interview. Or you may work yourself up to a state of anger before you attempt it. Because you're dealing with a nonpromotable who may already be resentful, defensive, and overly sensitive, disciplinary counseling can easily get out of control.

4. *Problem-Solving Counseling.* On-the-job and off-the-job problems are often brought to your attention by subordinates. Or you may initiate counseling when you recognize a problem that your subordinate doesn't see. In either case, the success of this kind of counseling depends on the ability of both the subordinate and yourself to work together to define the problem, gather facts, and consider options in selecting one you both agree is most likely to work.

5. *Development Counseling.* Unfortunately, many companies rarely, if ever, schedule development counseling for their nonpromotable employees. Its purpose is to enhance the personal growth of the subordinate. The questions it considers are as follows:

Are you using your personal skills to best advantage?
What new skills are you adding to help you perform better now and in the future?
What resources are available to help you with your development?
How can you help yourself?
What learning objectives should you set, and what learning activities should you plan?

Common Counseling Problems

Each type of formal counseling interview has its own problems. These problems can often be managed by following the basic strategies outlined below.

Instructional Counseling

In instructional interviews, the nonpromotable commonly resists attempts to teach him new skills or strengthen old skills. Sometimes he just doesn't want to learn. It takes effort and practice to acquire new skills, and he believes he has managed well enough without them in the past. He asks himself, "What's in it for me? Why should I learn?" You must address these questions before you attempt to give an instructional interview. Your strategic approach to the interview must take into consideration your subordinate's needs and the benefits that new learning offers. Rather than try to sell those benefits to your subordinate, involve him in a discussion in which he discovers that there are sound reasons to learn new skills.

Correcting well-entrenched work habits creates greater problems than trying to teach new skills. When a subordinate has a long history of doing something in a certain way, he not only feels comfortable with that method, he has an emotional investment in it. He doesn't want to admit that he's been doing things inefficiently. It's embarrassing and uncomfortable for him to do so. Before relearning can occur, he must first unlearn what he believes he knows. For this to happen, you must establish good rapport with him. This rapport depends on openness and trust. If he drops his defenses by recognizing his learning deficiencies and admitting not only that his level of competence is deteriorating, but that he is becoming obsolescent, he must be convinced that you will not misuse this information — you won't chide, embarrass, or punish him. Instead, you'll focus on helping him.

Evaluative Counseling

The common counseling problems associated with evaluative interviews often lead to severe confrontations. Your nonpromotable subordinate is sensitive to criticism. He regards even mild advice and suggestions as threats. He may choose to shut out criticism by not listening or by rejecting it totally by discounting your qualifications to give it. Often, he may appear to accept what's being said to him, whereas in reality he's ignoring it or hearing only what he wants to hear.

Several strategies will serve you well in coping with evaluative interviews. Most importantly, you must withhold your natural tendency to tell your subordinate what you think of him. Whereas a subordinate is delighted to hear positive judgments, he won't feel the same about the negative side. That's why it's highly desirable to encourage your subordinate to prepare for self-evaluation prior to the interview. He should review, in writing, what areas of his work are going well and in what areas he is less than satisfied. Ideally, he'll come to the interview having already identified specific problem areas. However, if his self-evaluation is a whitewash that covers up any deficiencies, you should try another tack. Show that you know what lies beneath the whitewash:

There are several things you did not discuss in your self-evaluation that are areas of concern to me. Perhaps you overlooked them or don't feel as concerned as I do about them. Would you give me your opinion about . . . ?

Then you state the facts as you see them and try to involve him in a discussion of the facts as if he were a disinterested third party. Draw him out; try to get him to express his feelings and opinions, and supply your own only when asked specifically to do so. Periodically during the discussion, check for mutual understanding by restating a point he made or asking him to clarify or summarize what he said. If the counseling interview has been successful, both of you will agree on problem areas and possible corrective actions.

Disciplinary Counseling

Whereas the evaluative interview may antagonize subordinates, disciplinary counseling may evoke much more than a flare of temper. It may drive a wedge between you and a subordinate and create a feud or grudge. Often, as an aftermath of a disciplinary interview, your subordinate will feel, "Foul! I'm innocent and have been punished unfairly." Even if he acknowledges guilt, he may feel that the punishment he received was too harsh.

You too may be dissatisfied with the disciplinary interview if you naively expect your subordinate to both accept punishment sheepishly and change his behavior. As every parent knows, boxing ears and denying privileges rarely produce desired end results.

The objective of disciplinary counseling should be to focus a spotlight on unacceptable conduct and to uncover the reasons for it. When a subordinate acts in a way he knows you will censor, he is willing to face the risk of punishment. He has decided that the benefits derived from his actions are worth the risk of punishment. It is your task to find out why he feels as he does, and then, with his active participation, search for areas of mutual satisfaction. After discussion, you may discover that your subordinate has good reason to act as he does. You may then decide to make changes yourself. Or he may discover that his own reasoning is faulty and agree willingly to modify his undesirable behavior.

Of course, when your subordinate has violated important rules of conduct, he should be given, and indeed expects, punishment. However, the punishment should "fit the crime," and its fairness should be discussed thoroughly. The purpose of punishment is not to release your anger, but to establish that there are clear boundaries of acceptable and unacceptable behavior. Punishment is intended to protect against future unacceptable acts rather than serve as an act of retribution.

Problem Solving

Unlike disiplinary counseling, a problem-solving interview has the advantage of not pitting you against your subordinate. Instead, you should schedule it because you genuinely want to help him. In fact, both your subordinate and you should want to resolve the problems as fast as possible. Unfortunately, that's where problem solving can go astray. You rush to solutions without sufficiently defining the problem and gathering facts. Acting in haste, you consider only a limited number of options.

Futhermore, some subordinates are so anxious to rid themselves of their problems that they dump them on you. For them, it's an ideal solution. They no longer have to worry about problems you have assumed, a common failing of non-promotables. They feel they have nothing to gain by trying to solve tough problems and prefer to sidestep or unload them. As a result, they become increasingly dependent on you, and you become overburdened with their problems.

Your strategy in handling problem-solving counseling should be to shift from solution centering to problem centering. Help the subordinate to define his problem, gather necessary facts, and search for alternatives. You serve as a process facilitator — you don't solve problems for your subordinates;

instead you help them to approach problem solving in a logical way. The responsibility for problem solving remains with the individual.

Developmental Counseling

Just as being overly helpful leads to failure in the problem-solving interview, it can destroy the effectiveness of developmental counseling. In this case the problem is that you try to assume responsibility for the development of the subordinate who is at a dead end. He's fearful he may go stale but is unwilling to develop himself unless he feels there's a solid payoff for his efforts. And for any self-development he does undertake he expects a fast return.

Your approach to developmental counseling is similar to that for problem-solving counseling inasmuch as you encourage your subordinate to assume the burden of his own development. Again, you act as facilitator. In this role, you can show your subordinate that anyone who doesn't grow in a rapidly changing work environment will find it difficult to just stand still. Most likely, he will slide backward at considerable personal cost to himself. Unfortunately, just telling him will not suffice. You have to help him take a longer-term view of his life and to deal with such questions as: Where am I going? What do I want to accomplish? What do I have to do to make things happen? What's likely to make me happy? This kind of life/career planning will lead to his recognition of a need for self-development.

THE COUNSELING INTERVIEW WORKSHEET

In conducting any one of the five types of counseling interviews, the Counseling Interview Worksheet (Worksheet 2) will help strengthen your counseling. Let's see how one manager uses it with a problematic subordinate.

The manager schedules a disciplinary counseling interview with Jane. It is held in his own office behind closed doors and with instructions left at the switchboard to hold phone calls. He uses the worksheet to state the purpose of the interview — to discuss the frequent arguments that Jane has been having with other members of the department.

WORKSHEET 2
Counseling interview.

Preinterview:

Date _____ *7/1/77* _____ Name _____ *Jane Reilly* _____

Type of Interview _____ *Disciplinary* _____

Location _____ *Office* _____

Purpose:

Jane has been involved in frequent arguments. Determine how to change her behavior.

Critical
incidents:

Feb. 1   Argument with J.L. over holiday schedule.
March 12 Argument with...over...
April 8   Argument with...over...
            .
            .
            .
June 20   Argument with...over...

Perceived problem(s):

Subordinate	Manager
Girls ganging up on her because they are cliquish and she's an outsider.	*She appears to be inflexible, argumentative, and tactless.*

Seriousness:

Some girls threatening to transfer. Productivity affected. Problem has been going on for six months. It involves whole department and is getting worse.

Past subordinate/manager relationship:

Gets along well with me. She's friendly and cooperative with me and is open and trusting.

Interview:

Reaction of subordinate: *Recognizes seriousness of problem and acknowledges own personality problems.*

Problem agreement: *She agrees that her behavior precipitates and escalates arguments.*

Alternatives:
- *Interpersonal relations training*
- *Restructuring of job to isolate from others*
- *Transfer*

Action agreement: *Interpersonal relations training*

Postinterview:

Expectations: *Reduced frequency of arguments and better acceptance by others.*

Follow-up: *Three months.*

Jane is an intelligent, highly competent assistant buyer for a major department store. She has extensive retailing experience and an excellent education, which includes an MBA. In the eight years she's been with her current firm, she worked her way up steadily, holding a variety of jobs. About three years ago, she was appointed assistant buyer. Since that time, Jane has been in three different departments, having been transferred each time by managers who felt she was disrupting their departments.

Without making any value judgments, her manager lists the critical incidents he has observed and those that have been reported to him, the dates of specific arguments, and the persons or issues involved.

Then in the section of the worksheet labeled Perceived Problem(s), the manager states them as seen through Jane's eyes and his own. Jane finds the other members of the department cliquish; they treat her as an outsider. Her manager feels that she may be inflexible, argumentative, and tactless (a preliminary and tentative judgment reached after reading her past personnel records and discussing the matter with her previous managers).

Next, he comments on the seriousness of the problem. How long has the problem been going on? How many people are involved in it? Is it getting worse or getting better? How much time does he feel he has to correct it?

In this particular situation, several of the women are threatening to transfer. The problem has been going on for at least six months. It involves the entire department and is getting progressively worse.

One last item completes the preinterview information. Under the heading Past Subordinate/Manager Relationship, he comments on the quality of his relationship with Jane. Because she had entered his department with a blemished record, Jane had been very careful to please her boss. She completed work assignments promptly and worked efficiently. She was always courteous and pleasant to him. Whenever they talked, she was open and trusting.

During the interview, the manager records whether or not differences in the perception of the problem have been resolved and what ideas were suggested by either the subordinate or himself as to possible courses of action. Finally, which specific actions do they both agree on? In this case, after an active discussion, Jane begins to realize that her feeling of being treated as an outsider is aggravated by her own behavior. They consider three different courses of action: special training in interpersonal relations, a restructuring of her job so that she can restrict her contact with the other members of the department, or transfer to another department. They decide that she needs special training to deal with her personality shortcomings — they were responsible for her problems in the past, and they would continue to be so in the future no matter where she worked. Therefore, special training in interpersonal relations is scheduled, and her manager discusses with her the consequences of not giving a full commitment to the agreed-on action.

After the interview, the manager completes the last part of the worksheet. He comments on the reaction of Jane to the counseling session and on his expectations for future improvement. He feels that Jane recognizes the seriousness of the situation and is beginning to understand her personality problems. However, he doesn't try to fool himself as to what might or might not be changed. He knows that she is capable of modest behavioral changes but cannot overcome a life-long style of behavior. He will be satisfied with a reduction in the frequency of arguments and some indications of better acceptance of Jane in the department. Finally, he schedules a follow-up interview to take place in three months at which time he will discuss Jane's feelings about the training she is receiving, her relationships with the other people in the department, and feedback from them about her.

The worksheet is certainly helpful, but it's a valuable tool only in the hands of someone who understands some of the basic do's and don'ts of counseling. The following examples demonstrate how an inexperienced counselor and an experienced counselor conduct an interview with Jane.

INEXPERIENCED COUNSELOR

Jane: Those women have been ganging up on me since I started working here. They've worked together for a long time and because I'm a newcomer, they treat me like an outsider.

Supervisor: I can't believe that. They're a nice bunch of women who are friendly to everybody. You must have done something to rub them the wrong way. Besides, I've seen how argumentative you can get and you certainly can be very hard-nosed in dealing with people. I don't like to tell you this, but I think you have some personality problems. If you expect to stay in this department, you are going to have to learn how to bend. Look at Sue. She hasn't been in the department much longer than you, and yet she seems well accepted.

Violating all basic principles of counseling, the supervisor attacks Jane's personality directly instead of focusing on her behavior. He lectures her as though she were a little girl without trying to understand her point of view. He threatens her. He belittles her by making unfavorable comparisons with a peer in the department.

EXPERIENCED COUNSELOR

Supervisor: Jane, I'm concerned about the number of arguments that have taken place in the department during the last six months. Here are specific arguments that I've observed personally or that have been reported to me.

[*He goes on to give the details as to the persons involved in the arguments with Jane and the issues as reported or observed.*]

Are these points correct?

Jane: Yes, those arguments did take place, and the reasons for the arguments are stated correctly. But none of them were my fault. Those women in the department have it in for me.

Supervisor: Can you tell me more about that?

Jane: [*Explains the situation as she sees it.*]

Supervisor: I can fully appreciate your concern. You feel that you're an outsider and that the others pick on you.

Jane: That's right. That's exactly how I see it.

Supervisor: That's strange. I've known most of those women for a long time, and normally they're friendly. They have not had similar difficulties with others in the past. Is there something about your approach to them that may have contributed in some way to the situation?

Jane: I don't know what you mean.

Supervisor: Let me give you an example from my own personal observation. You had an argument with Arlene about whose turn it was to work during the upcoming holiday. It appeared to me that she was willing to make some concessions, but you weren't willing to make any. What do you think?

[*At first Jane starts to defend herself; slowly she begins to acknowledge that her own actions may have contributed to the problem. But she becomes emotional.*]

Jane: Maybe I was short-tempered and I did want my own way, but I haven't been wrong in all those arguments . . . .

[*She goes on to explain her side of each argument. By the time she finishes explaining, she's shouting at the manager; finally she bursts into tears.*]

Supervisor: From what you've said, I fully appreciate the amount of discomfort you must have felt and can better understand some of the actions you've taken. But it's my responsibility to restore good working relationships within the department. Instead of focusing on who is to blame, is there anything we might be able to do to improve the situation?

Using good counseling techniques, the manager listens to Jane's point of view, shows interest in her, doesn't allow his own emotions to be provoked by her's, allows her to save face, focuses on facts and problems, and tries to get Jane to participate in developing possible solutions. And throughout the interview, he tries to draw her out by use of indirect questioning: "Tell me more about that." "How do you feel about that?"

He also explains that although he understands her position, he still has a responsibility to restore harmony in the department; without threatening her, he makes it apparent that he intends to do so. He works continually to shift from a blame-fixing mode to a problem-solving mode.

SELF-EVALUATION
of COUNSELING CHARACTERISTICS

Many managers believe that because they have had many opportunities to counsel subordinates that they are skilled at it. However, they probably haven't stopped to evaluate themselves systematically. The counseling self-evaluation ratings shown in Worksheet 3 are valuable in that they give you an opportunity to rate yourself for 15 characteristics that are essential to effective counseling.

WORKSHEET 3
Counseling self-evaluation ratings.

CHARACTERISTICS	HIGH 5	4	3	2	LOW 1
Analytical skills					
Communicative skills					
Judgment					
Frankness					
Calmness					
Accepting					
Tact					
Preparedness					
Consistency					
Empathy					
Flexibility					
Problem-solving skills					
Negotiation skills					
Trusting					
Controlling skills					

When completing the ratings, the manager should ask himself the following questions:

Analytical ability. In a counseling situation, how quickly do you get to the heart of the problem? Are you able to strip away irrelevancies and ambiguities? Do you recognize underlying facts hidden by your emotions?

How effective are your communicative skills? Do you know how to listen carefully? Can you explain yourself clearly and concisely? Do you understand the significance of body language and facial expressions? Do you know how to ask meaningful questions, particularly indirect and open-ended questions? Do you check for understanding by using such techniques as reflection, restatement, and clarification?

How reliable is your judgment? Do you pass judgment prematurely? Do you base your judgment on facts? How do your predispositions influence your judgment? Do you explore all facets of a problem before you make a judgment?

Frankness. Are you completely honest during the interview? Are you open? Do you tell it "like it is"? Can you give criticism without being apologetic?

Do you remain calm during the interview? Should it become stressful and a subordinate gets angry, do you control yourself? Do you allow other people's emotions to rattle you?

How accepting are you? Do you start the interview with a genuine desire to help? Are you tolerant of other people's differences? Do you display genuine interest and respect for a subordinate you don't like? Are you patient and understanding?

How tactful are you? Can you criticize without hurting? Can you take an unpopular position without alienating? Are you careful in expressing disapproval, disbelief, contradiction, and threat?

Do you prepare carefully for counseling sessions? Are you thorough in your fact gathering? Are you aware of the importance of proper timing? Do you select settings that are quiet and free of interruption?

How consistent are you in counseling interviews? Do you reverse your positions? Can you be depended on to stand firm on what you say? Do you act like "one of the boys" and then back off and use authority as a defense?

How empathic are you? Can you put yourself in the other person's shoes to see his point of view? Are you able to feel his concerns? Do you address his needs rather than yours?

How flexible are you? Once you take a position, are you able to change it in the face of convincing evidence? Do you start an interview with your mind made up?

Do you have good problem-solving skills? Do you know how to go about specifying a problem, gathering facts, developing and evaluating alternatives?

How good are your negotiation skills? Do you know how to negotiate for behavioral changes? How successful are you at arriving at reasonable settlements?

How trusting and how trustful are you? Are you willing to

depend on the honesty of subordinates? Can they depend on yours?

Do you maintain control of the counseling interview? Does it get mired down in irrelevancies, or do you direct it toward a logical conclusion? Are you careful not to talk too much? Do you know how to make proper use of silence?

FAILURES in COUNSELING

As mentioned earlier in this chapter, a prime reason for counseling failure is a lack of preparation — you allow yourself to participate in spontaneous and unplanned counseling. Even when you schedule formal interviews, you treat them too casually with the feeling that you can conduct them without too much "fuss and bother." If you're too busy to give proper time and attention to a counseling interview, you're better off not scheduling it.

Another source of failure may be your reluctance to serve as a counselor. You may feel uncomfortable in the role, fearful of confrontations and embarrassed by emotions. Accordingly, you rush the interview and appear uninterested. Any discussion is superficial.

Contributing to many failures may be the fact that you don't really want to help all subordinates. You've grown to dislike some of them. So instead of maintaining a neutral stance during the interview, you conduct it as if you were an adversary and punish rather than help.

Inability to address a subordinate's problems is another source of failure. You schedule an interview in order to correct a particular problem. During the session your subordinate poses other problems that are more meaningful to him. Rather than discuss them, you may persist in pursuing your own interests. This results in what Richard M. Greene, Jr. calls a duolog.[*] You and your subordinate take turns not talking to each other. Each of you is following your own thoughts.

Poor timing often leads to failure. You may wait too long to schedule a counseling interview thereby causing the situation

[*]Richard M. Greene, Jr., *The Management Game: How to Win With People* (Homewood, Ill.: Dow-Irwin, 1969), p. 100.

to escalate out of control. When you schedule an interview hastily, you may give undue importance to a problem that would have resolved itself without your interference. Sometimes you may schedule an interview when the subordinate is unprepared psychologically for it. He's too emotional to listen to reason. You should have scheduled it after a reasonable cool-off period.

Ironically, the manager who takes too active a role in a counseling interview often fails. You may talk too much, give advice too freely, bombard your subordinate with questions, and be too directive. Perhaps you can't stand the sound of silence and need to fill it with your own voice. An effective counselor plays a much more passive role; he encourages his subordinate to talk and to work out his own problems. He functions as a creative listener trying to understand not only what is said, but what is not said.

Counseling cannot succeed when a manager has unrealistic expectations. Perhaps you expect your subordinate to undergo major behavioral changes after a single counseling interview. Or you're impatient when a subordinate doesn't talk freely or isn't completely cooperative. You may expect the interview to proceed in a certain way and get upset when it doesn't.

It is particularly disconcerting when a manager experiences failure using a counseling approach that has worked well in the past. You may not have taken into account the individuality of the person being counseled. Sometimes all the rules of counseling have to be thrown out the window in dealing with some subordinates. You have to feel your way through the counseling interview. When methods don't seem to be working, you should abandon them and try others. Like commanding an artillery battery, you fire successive salvos, observing proximity to the target and gradually zeroing in.

Terminating an interview too quickly will lead to failure. Each counseling interview should serve to improve mutual understanding and agreement. If it doesn't, the time has been wasted. In a single interview, the amount of improvement may be modest, but at least it should be a step in the right direction. Managers often feel that just because they have told subordinates what they intended, they can conclude an interview without checking to find out if they have gotten through at all.

Some men and women take nonpromotability in stride. But they are the exceptions. Most, to some extent, are affected adversely.

From a humanistic point of view as well as for sound business reasons, you have a responsibility to help subordinates accept the fact that they will not be promoted and to adapt successfully to it. Planned, systematic, well-conducted counseling provides the help they need. Its value is aptly described by one man who received meaningful counseling when he needed it most:

Even though I was in the process of becoming nonpromotable for several years, when I finally admitted it to myself I was shaken up. I had trouble sleeping, I was irritable, and I lost my appetite. My wife became so concerned, she asked me to see a doctor. I told her there was nothing wrong with me and that I'd get over it. But I didn't.

At first my work performance wasn't affected. Then it started to deteriorate. That's when my boss scheduled a series of counseling interviews. During the first one, I didn't have much to say. And although my boss tried, he couldn't get me to open up. However, I did get the feeling that he wanted to help and was interested in me. In subsequent interviews we started to talk—or I should say I started to talk and he listened. Most of the time all he did was nod his head and check with me to see if he completely understood what I was saying. I had expected him to give me the same useless advice all my friends and relatives had given me. But he didn't.

I'm not even sure why, but after three counseling interviews I really opened up. It just felt good to get it all off my chest. I even told him I had lost interest in my job and had started to goof off. But he didn't bat an eye. After half a dozen interviews, we started working together to help me make plans to overcome my problems. And then he helped me to start thinking about the future and some of the things I might do to make my job more enjoyable.

Maybe without my boss I would have adapted eventually by myself. Who knows? But I'm convinced that without his help I couldn't have made the adaptation nearly as fast.

CHAPTER THREE

Development— An Investment or a Waste?

Why should a manager invest time developing people who will not be promoted? They've been in their present jobs long enough to know what to do. And they'll probably stay in these same jobs, so why prepare them for future responsibilities? Or build up their hopes by involving them in a development program? Besides, many nonpromotables would rather not be bothered. Many managers believe their time would be better spent developing people for whom it may mean advancement.

Managers are rightfully concerned about making an investment in nonpromotables that could bring no returns. However, they may be making some false assumptions. For example, you may assume that somebody who's been in a job for several years knows how to perform that job fully. That's a dangerous assumption. Over the years a subordinate has probably acquired many bad work habits and mishandles at least some aspects of his job. His errors are often invisible because he chooses to hide them from his boss using such common practices as faking, covering up, and taking shortcuts. Furthermore, he may be attending to the "things" aspects of his job, but failing in its "people" aspects. The following two case histories show how managers can be misled by subordinates.

Ellen is the office manager in a busy real estate brokerage office. She joined the firm eleven years ago, and three years ago was appointed office manager in charge of a clerical staff of six women. She likes her job and has no aspirations beyond her present position.

On the surface, it appears that she runs an efficient office. However, a smaller staff under a better supervisor could easily handle the same work load. Ellen hasn't tried to acquire managerial skills and provides only token leadership. Thus, her subordinates like her, but don't respect her. Because she's weak, they don't perform well and tend to take advantage of her.

Irv is the senior purchasing agent for a large plastics company. Having spent most of his 25-year work career in the purchasing departments of several companies, he knows his specialty. In his current position, he has earned the reputation of getting his company "the most for its money." What his management overlooks is that he is hard to work for and with. He delegates little to his subordinates, makes little attempt to train them, is intolerant of any mistakes, and is often short-tempered and disagreeable. When dealing with suppliers, he's a tyrant. Because they want the company's business, suppliers put up with his impossible demands. However, if there are any opportunities to get back at him without jeopardizing the business, they do so. Over the years, his approach to people has caused costly turnover of staff and suppliers.

Another false assumption you may make is that a subordinate is necessarily nonpromotable. Someone you believe has reached his or her capacity may be able to grow into higher-level responsibilities. This individual may not meet the ideal qualifications for the next career step, but may have qualities that more than compensate for other shortcomings. Also, the qualifications for the next-level job may have been set unrealistically high. For example, it's common practice to require advanced college degrees for jobs that could be performed by talented people with less formal education.

By developing the skills of subordinates, whether or not you believe they are nonpromotable, you avoid possible errors in judgment about their capabilities in addition to protecting their competence. Individuals don't stay the same. They are always in the process of becoming better or worse. When their managers lose interest in them, subordinates tend to lose interest in their jobs. This leads to indifference and dissatisfaction and ultimately to a loss of competence. This sliding backward was vividly described to me by a group leader in a chemicals processing plant:

My feelings that my boss had lost interest in me didn't develop overnight. At first I was aware of the fact that he spent less time with me and more time with some of the other men. During the time he spent with me, we usually exchanged social pleasantries instead of talking about the job. When things went wrong, he came around to find out what had happened, but otherwise he left me alone. I became increasingly concerned about the lack of attention so I confronted him. He told me that he had confidence in me and that I did not require close supervision. He asked jokingly if I really wanted him to pester me. Of course I didn't. What I wanted was the feeling that he cared about me as an individual. Also, I realized afterward, I needed active interaction with him to keep me motivated and challenged.

Feeling neglected and forgotten, I lost interest in my job. I stopped reading trade journals, attending association meetings, and talking to suppliers about new equipment and techniques. I didn't care about keeping up to date. As you would expect, it didn't take long for me to become rusty.

Subordinates — promotable and nonpromotable — want and need attention. Their job satisfaction and value to the company can be increased by helping them to make the best use of their talents. By investing time in their development, you appeal to the whole person and have a better chance of getting a whole-hearted effort. You'll have to settle for getting less from subordinates if you waste their untapped talent and the rich resource of their individual experience. Unless you can answer the following questions with complete assurance, you are probably not appealing to your subordinates as whole persons:

Do you have an accurate inventory of the talents your subordinates have displayed in their current and past jobs?

Are you fully aware of talents displayed by subordinates off the job?

Are your subordinates completely involved with their jobs, giving their full energy and enthusiasm voluntarily?

Are your subordinates continually trying to improve themselves?

Do your subordinates search for better ways to do things?

Are your subordinates actively interested in their work, finding it a source of satisfaction?

Do your subordinates give you their complete cooperation?

Are your subordinates willing to invest time and energy today in the belief that you will reward them appropriately in the future?

Are your subordinates committed to high work standards?

Are your subordinates loyal to you and the company?

Do your subordinates show initiative, imagination, and creativity?

Are your subordinates unwilling to compromise the quality of their work through shortcuts?

Have you displayed a genuine interest in the future of your subordinates?

The old saying, "You get back what you give," has special meaning in the relationship between a manager and a nonpromotable subordinate. An investment in developing their full talents and capabilities will reap rich returns.

TRAINING vs. DEVELOPMENT

One reason for the reluctancy of managers to invest in development is that they equate "training" and "development." They consider development to be nothing more than allowing subordinates to attend training programs offered by company or outside organizations.

The differences between training and development are summarized in Figure 2. Let's examine these differences more closely.

Whereas development may include participation in formal training programs, its scope is much broader than that of training. The objective of training is to improve skills in a specific area. Its content may or may not be appropriate for the needs of a particular individual in his or her own work environment. In contrast, development is designed to fill individual needs within specific job environments. In fact, the first step in an effective development program is to diagnose specific individual needs. Thereafter, its goal involves making basic behav-

FIGURE 2
Comparison of training and development.

FACTORS	TRAINING	DEVELOPMENT
Scope	Narrow	Broad
Emphasis	Skills acquisition	Behavioral change
Orientation	Subject	Problem
Methods	Classroom and "canned"	Guided and individualized experiences
Learner role	Passive	Active
Direction	Teacher	Self
Time perspective	Present and short term	Future and long term
Transferability to job	Uncertain	Certain
Anxiety level	High	Low
Participation	Usually involuntary	Voluntary

ioral changes. Through the process of development, the nonpromotable learns how to better cope with his changing work environment. He learns to evaluate himself in terms of work habits, attitudes, values, emotional responses, expectations, and sources of satisfaction. Most importantly, he learns when and how to change.

Unlike training, which has a subject orientation, development consists in problem orientation. In the training situation, someone else has decided what an individual should know; the learner sits back passively as the trainer attempts to force-feed the proper knowledge and skills. In a development program, the individual recognizes a problem and wants to do something about it. He takes the initiative and plans a program of action. His boss is a resource for whatever help he feels he needs. He sets the pace and directs the action.

Because training is teacher directed, it's most efficient when conducted in a classroom where a teacher can have direct contact with a group. These students either are selected or volunteer as candidates for instruction in a specific subject. Wherever possible, "canned" material is used and reused with new groups to avoid the cost of creating new materials.

Development is not bound to the classroom. It takes place on the job in unstructured situations. Whatever materials are used by the learner are personally selected from a variety of resources. For some learning activities he may want and need individual attention from people with special expertise. For other learning activities he can rely completely on himself. Thus the development program of one individual will be very different from that of another. What works for one individual may not work for another. And of course the reverse is true.

Another essential difference between training and development involves time perspectives. Training is a series of related or unrelated individual events with discrete time limits. Its purpose is to provide short-term skills, generally for use in one's present job. A development program may also yield short-term benefits, but its focus is on long-term rewards. Development is a process that continues throughout one's career.

As time passes, the scheduling of training events for nonpromotables usually becomes less frequent. They have mastered most of the skills they need in order to perform their current jobs. They believe "they don't need any more training," and they may equate formal training with "being treated like a beginner." When forced to attend prescribed courses, some become anxious and afraid to compete with newer, younger colleagues. Many, uncertain of the relevance of new skills, approach learning experiences with indifference and lack of interest. They don't like to be away from their job and home; they show their displeasure by refusing to learn what is taught or by resisting its use on the job.

Because development is voluntary and less anxiety-producing than training, it tends to be far more stimulating and satisfying to the learner; his new skills are more likely to be applied on the job. He has chosen what he feels he needs to learn; and he controls the pace and content. He doesn't have to compete with anybody as he would in a classroom. Furthermore, because the burden of development rests on his own shoulders he feels he's being treated as a responsible adult.

CONSIDERING the WHOLE PERSON

When you're responsible for training someone, you don't have to know much about his background. But when you assume responsibility to help someone with his development, you need much more information about him. Many variables affect the choice of initial development projects and the pace, sequencing, and scheduling of projects thereafter. Your emphasis should be placed on self-development for your subordinate. You serve as a facilitator who helps him overcome the initial inertia that prevents subordinates from launching self-development programs. You provide objectivity, insights, and the benefits of your own experience. Your continuing interest and guidance are essential to the success of any development program.

By knowing the background of your subordinates, you will better perform your function as facilitator. The need for such knowledge is dramatized by the following case histories. (Note in the first case the forces that work against development and in the second case the forces that work for it.)

Case One

John's not going anywhere in his company, and he doesn't care. In fact, he's surprised about the amount of forward progress he has made. He has a better job than most of his friends and all his relatives. He is the only member of his immediate family to have gone to college. And even he wouldn't have gone to college except for the fact that he had won a football scholarship. After college, he was drafted into the Army where he had an undistinguished career, rising to the rank of corporal.

After discharge, one of the friends he had made in the service convinced him to join his current company. Because he was naturally competitive, he had received two promotions within five years. But, as he identified with a group of "old-timers," he lost his drive. The members of the group had, as they put it, "dropped out of the rat race years ago." They enjoyed each other's comradery both on and off the job, and spent much time socializing during the work day, managing to work as little as possible. But, if anyone in the group was reprimanded for his work habits, they all supported their colleague by becoming hostile and uncooperative toward the manager. As a result, there was an unspoken agreement between them and him: "Don't bother us or expect too much from us, and we'll meet minimally acceptable standards."

Since John and his colleagues were senior men, they didn't respond well to the idea of training. To their minds training was nonsense and of no practical value. And John personally distrusted any suggestion that he consider self-development. He felt that his boss was trying to manipulate him into sacrificing his personal time for the benefit of the company.

Case Two

Mary, an employee in the same company, holds very different attitudes and values. She comes from a background of high achievers, and her associations were with people with similar backgrounds. Even though she admits she has reached the top of her career, she still feels determined to improve herself and "make the most of her job." She's not satisfied with anything but top performance.

In the past, whenever she attended formal training classes, she did so with enthusiasm and tried to learn and apply everything she was taught. In recent years the frequency of her being scheduled for formal training has declined, so she has taken the responsibility for her own self-development. She reads trade literature and books, observes others whose performance she would like to emulate, has a healthy intellectual curiosity that prompts her to ask questions frequently and to experiment with new techniques, and consults often with others from whom she feels she can learn.

Obviously, the approach to developing John will be quite different from that for Mary because she has embarked on a campaign of self-development and needs only encouragement and support. But John needs much more guidance and help.

He, like many nonpromotables, neither wants nor believes he needs development.

In personal interviews I've talked with others like John who expressed their resistance to development saying, "What's the use? I'm content with things as they are and don't want to be bothered. Sure, I want more from my job, but I feel I would have to pay too much of a price for the extras. And even if I were willing to make a personal investment, I'm not sure what I would get in return."

Some felt that they shouldn't have to develop themselves and probably couldn't if they wanted to. They believed that someone in the company (they weren't sure who) should assume responsibility for their development. These people resented the absence of programs, but they did not have a clear idea of what development was all about or whether they even needed it. A typical attitude was: "I want to solve my own problems. I don't like any interference and want to be left alone. I know what's best for me. And nobody around here is really qualified to help me." After such strong statements about independence, they would say, "In other companies they don't leave you on the beach. They do all sorts of things for their people. They care if you're dissatisfied with what you're doing. They give you a reason to take pride in your job and yourself. They want to bring out the best in you. I wish things were different at my company."

Although the number of interviews I conducted was insufficient to give statistically significant information, there was no question in my mind that all of the interviewees:

Were uncertain as to the meaning of development
Were uncertain as to the respective developmental roles of themselves and their bosses
Believed that their companies were not doing much to help them to develop
Felt their companies should be interested in their futures

THE HAPPY and the UNHAPPY NONPROMOTABLE

A first-line field sales manager, in discussing one of the salesmen under his supervision, reacted as follows to the suggestion that he consider developing all his subordinates, nonpromotables included:

You said I should be concerned about the development of all the men under my supervision. What about a man like Charlie? He's happy being a salesman. He loves his job. He makes a decent living and has a satisfying life. I don't want to ruin a good thing. Don't I run the risk of changing his positive attitudes by forcing him to rethink his life and his future?

Many managers are prompted by a desire to maintain the status quo. Subordinates appear to be content and working hard. So why jeopardize the existing harmony? No reason, if the following questions can be answered with an unqualified "yes":

Are your subordinates as satisfied with their jobs as they were when they first started?

Will they be as satisfied five years from now? Ten years from now?

Will their changing work and home environments affect their job satisfaction?

Are there any changes in the job or their personal lives that might give them greater satisfaction?

Job satisfaction is not a fixed entity. It is subject to wide swings, upward and downward, depending on the interplay of many different satisfiers and dissatisfiers on and off the job. Even employees who appear to be completely satisfied may be troubled by persistent sources of dissatisfaction. The ideal job just doesn't exist. And even if it did, it's unlikely that it would remain ideal indefinitely, managing to satisfy all one's needs.

The potential for dissatisfaction with one's job is especially great for the nonpromotable. He stays in the same job long enough for some of his past satisfiers to lose their strength. Yet new dissatisfiers are emerging — work that used to be interesting becomes uninteresting. Positive relationships with peers and supervisors are disrupted as people move up and out of the company. The job may become overly demanding or not demanding enough, depending on conditions beyond his control. What was originally novelty may become routine. Performance that won him praise and advancement in the past, measured by different standards, may become unrecognized, unrewarded, and even criticized. Talents that had served him well in the past may not serve the needs of the future. The delicate balance of variables that encourage satisfaction is constantly changing. And for the nonpromotable, that balance is more likely to change for worse than better.

Development will help the nonpromotable cope with emerging sources of dissatisfaction. By developing, he grows in his capacity to adapt successfully and function effectively in the work environment. He learns how to modify his attitudes, values, and emotional responses. He fine-tunes his performance and acquires new knowledge and skills as needed. Development is essential in the dynamic work environment. It enhances performance and fights dissatisfaction. It should be of vital concern to the individual and to you as manager.

METHODS of DEVELOPMENT

Hopefully, you're convinced that everyone needs development throughout his or her career, especially the nonpromotable. Agreement to a lifetime commitment is the important first step in any development program. Commitment leads naturally to continuing self-diagnosis and the search for learning experiences that coincide with developmental needs. In his book *The Adult Learner: A Neglected Species,* Malcolm Knowles says that adults are ready to learn things they need rather than ought.° In his opinion, the change from dependency to increasing self-directedness is the point at which one becomes "psychologically adult."

Guided Experience

The following case history illustrates how one man diagnosed his developmental problems and needs and arranged for appropriate learning experiences.

Gene is the personnel manager in a company that employs

°Malcolm Knowles, *The Adult Learner: A Neglected Species* (Houston: Gulf Publishing Co., 1973), p. 47.

250 people. With only clerical support, he administers a complex program that ranges from routine salary administration to active involvement in union negotiations. It was in the latter area that he diagnosed a personal problem. Until a few years ago, the union had been loosely organized within the company. At that point, the local unions representing the employees became affiliated with a powerful national union. Within the company, the union representatives became much better organized and more professional in their negotiations. In fact, in the last two years, Gene felt that he had not adequately represented company interests in union negotiations. In a recent series of run-ins with union leadership, he had become painfully aware of his deficiencies.

Having diagnosed an important problem, he recognized a need to develop better negotiation skills. He started to read literature on the subject, attended a seminar given by a leading expert, and discussed the problem with colleagues in other companies. These preliminary learning experiences provided new knowledge and some insights but, in his opinion, were not enough to make a substantial difference in his performance. Since nobody within the organization could give him additional guidance, he brought in a consultant to help him plan a more effective union relations program and to assist him in upcoming contract negotiations. However, as he explained to the consultant, he didn't want to dump his own responsibilities on a third party. He needed somebody who would serve the role of an informed critic and who could help him to develop his own skills. At the union contract negotiations, the expert maintained a low profile. He observed and offered suggestions and feedback only when asked for them by Gene. On only one occasion did he have to intervene more actively to prevent Gene from making a major mistake. This guided experience gave Gene new confidence, and within a short period of time, he no longer needed the help of an outside expert.

Another kind of guided experience that is helpful to development is initiated by one's manager. Usually he feels that a subordinate hasn't diagnosed a problem and doesn't recognize a developmental need. Therefore, he may decide to arrange a learning experience where he's more likely to see his problems and developmental needs. For example, Ted, an old-timer in a large printing plant, has become increasingly intolerant of newcomers. He's abrupt and impatient with them and expects them to be able to perform immediately like seasoned veterans.

His manager was concerned about this attitude. He felt Ted could make a major contribution in helping the newcomers, but his attitude was preventing him. In an effort to get him to assume a more helpful role, he suggested a work project. He asked Ted to plan an orientation program for newly hired people. To make sure that the program would be functional, he asked him to consider the problems of the orientation facilitator as well as the person being oriented. How could the orientation be made more acceptable to both of them? What special incentives might be built into the program?

Delighted with having been given a special project, which he interpreted as a sign of recognition, Ted plunged into developing the program. As he reviewed the problems, he began to appreciate some of his own shortcomings in working with newcomers. By the time he finished the project, he had changed his attitudes and responded to inexperienced people with greater understanding and tolerance.

Progressive Desensitization

When it's not convenient or practical to involve a subordinate in an actual work project, simulation may be a valid alternative. By simulating reality, you place your subordinate in a position wherein he is able to see problems and recognize needs under conditions that approximate reality. Ideally, you'll structure the simulation in a way that will reinforce desirable behaviors.

For example, in a counseling interview, Doris told her manager that she was having difficulty disciplining one of her subordinates because she was intimidated by direct confrontations with people. Her manager asked her if she would be interested in trying to develop better skills in handling confrontation by using a progressive desensitization process. He explained that she could gradually work her way up to han-

dling direct confrontations by first practicing them in simulated situations, starting with some very easy ones and then
harder ones. Every day they role-played confrontations and
then discussed how she felt she handled them. If she was dissatisfied, they would replay it so that she could try alternative
approaches. Although the confrontations were simulated, they
evoked her usual feelings of intimidation, particularly because her boss played his part realistically.

By the end of the week, she felt comfortable coping with her
feelings. In fact, after handling several of these confrontations
very successfully and receiving enthusiastic praise from her
boss, she even looked forward to them. Finally, she told her
boss she was ready to handle the discipline problem with her
subordinate. He suggested that they first role-play the situation so that she could practice her responses. Relatively little
practice was necessary because she handled the situation very
well. So when she called in her subordinate for a disciplinary
interview, she handled it with relative ease. The desensitization had succeeded in ridding her of feelings of intimidation.
She was calm and in complete control of the interview, even
though her subordinate had gotten emotional.

Modeling for Development

Another effective development technique that can be either
self-initiated or manager-initiated is the use of modeling.
Once a problem is diagnosed and a need recognized, someone
who handles similar problems well is selected as a model and
asked to describe his technique in detail. If possible, opportunities for direct observation should be planned. For example,
here's a situation in which modeling helped overcome a long-
term problem. Everybody joked about Ron's desk. It was
always a mess. He didn't mind the needling, but he was concerned because he realized he wasted time because he was
disorganized.

As a result, he worked longer hours than many of his colleagues and felt he didn't accomplish as much. He asked himself, "Who has the cleanest desk around here and yet has a
reputation for turning out a lot of work?" He identified one
man he believed to be highly efficient and who was also likely

to want to help him. Together they discussed the problems Ron had been having and compared their respective work habits. From these comparisons, Ron discovered several good ideas to eliminate time-wasters. He also asked permission of his boss to spend a few days working side by side with his colleague. By the end of the period of observation, he had pages of notes containing a wealth of ideas.

Additional Methods

In addition to the methods described, there are daily opportunities for development that arise in the process of doing one's job — asking questions, testing new ways of doing things, exposing oneself to new situations and new activities, consulting with specialists — the list is endless for the individual determined to overcome problems that are creating difficulties and learning skills he needs to possess.

DEVELOPMENTAL INTERVIEW

Regardless of the methods used, it's important for you to check regularly on the progress your subordinates are making. Worksheet 4 can be helpful in measuring progress. The questions are designed to provoke an active discussion between your subordinate and you.

1. *What do you believe are the most important aspects of your job?* Does your subordinate know what's expected of him? Are you both in complete agreement? If not, in what areas do you have significant disagreement? Are your priorities the same?

2. *How well do you perform the main functions of your job?* Do your subordinate and you agree on the ratings? Is there general disagreement or only in specific items? What evidence do you have to support your position? If there is substantial disagreement, why?

3. *For those things you believe you don't do well, what's getting in your way?* Are there any things beyond your subordinate's control that are interfering with his performance? Are there any reasons why he may not want to do these things well? Is there any pressure on him to rush them and thereby compromise performance quality?

WORKSHEET 4
Developmental interview.

What do you consider the most important aspects of your job?

How well do you perform the main functions of your job?

Self-rating	Manager's rating

For those things you believe you don't do well, what's getting in your way?

Have you improved last year in any of the performance areas you identified as problem areas?

What changes would you like to make in your job?

Would you need additional learning experiences to perform better in problem areas?

How could your skills and experience be better utilized?

How can you help develop yourself in the future?

I agree to	My manager agrees to

4. *Have you improved last year in any of the performance areas you identified as problem areas?* In what ways did he improve? What prompted him to improve? What kind of help did he get from you and others?

5. *What changes would you like to make in your job?* Why would he want to make these changes? How will they benefit him and the company? What's holding him back from making these changes?

6. *Would you need additional learning experiences to perform better in problem areas?* What kinds of learning experiences would be best? Who, within the company or outside it, might be able to give him assistance? How long might it take before he could upgrade his performance?

7. *How could your skills and experience be better utilized?* Are there any things he isn't doing that he believes he should? Are there any things that he does infrequently which he believes he should be doing more frequently? Why does he think his talents are not being put to better use?

8. *How can you help develop yourself in the future?* This question is designed to involve your subordinate and you in a learning contract. Your subordinate agrees to take part in specific, measurable learning activities to be completed within agreed-on time periods. You commit yourself to provide resources as needed, full cooperation, as well as necessary time and opportunities for him to apply his new knowledge and skills. The learning contract spells out learning objectives, tasks, and evidence of their accomplishment. For example: "In order to keep up to date, I agree to read a minimum of one important article in trade journals each week for the next three months. From each article, I will abstract at least one idea that I will put to work on the job in maintaining a journal that describes how I used the idea and the subsequent results."

After your subordinate completes his part of the learning contract, you should describe your role. For example: "I agree to allow my subordinate to experiment with new ideas and shall rely on his best judgment that whatever he tries will be mutually beneficial to himself and the company. However, I shall be available for assistance and shall expect periodic progress reports."

Questions 1 through 7 should be completed prior to the developmental interview and submitted to you at least one week in advance of a scheduled interview. This will give you an opportunity to complete your part of question 2. In doing this, you should indicate areas of agreement. No comment should be made about the ratings with which you disagree. Later, during the actual interview, you should explain that you withheld comments on some of the ratings until you could learn more about the basis for them.

During the interview itself, you should encourage your subordinate to explain his answer to each question fully. You will probably have to help him expand his responses by probing them. At times, he may resist attempts to be drawn out by saying, "I don't know what else to tell you," or "I really have nothing else to add." When this happens, you might consider using a "laundry list" question. This kind of question describes the kind of information that you are seeking and makes it more difficult for the subordinate to give general responses. For example:

> *Subordinate:* I can't think of any changes I want to make in my job. It seems alright as is.
>
> *Manager:* I'm pleased to hear that you are satisfied with your job. However, very few people believe that they have perfect jobs. I know I don't. How do you feel about such things as the amount of freedom of action you have, the pressures put on you, possibly annoying or unnecessary tasks, and any aspects of your job that may be monotonous?

The formal developmental interview should be scheduled at least once a year. Informal developmental discussions should be held regularly throughout the year. Many of these discussions will involve progress reports on learning activities contracted for in the developmental interview. Unforeseen difficulties may have been encountered, time commitments may not have been met, or your subordinate may have second thoughts about his developmental needs. Whether formal or informal, the important thing is that you maintain continuing dialog with your subordinate. Although he should assume responsibility for his own development, he'll benefit from your support, interest, and encouragement.

Thus, development is an investment the nonpromotable

must make in himself—his personal growth and future. Since this investment is in the best interest of himself and the company, it's your responsibility to help make it pay off. You serve as catalyst and as facilitator. Most importantly, you must demonstrate that you want your subordinate to grow and achieve job satisfaction.

CHAPTER FOUR

Revitalizing Stale People and Stale Jobs

As a manager, you have surely observed the enthusiasm and commitment of someone in a new job. He devours new learning experiences. He works hard without complaint. He uses his existing talents fully and wants to acquire new ones. He welcomes guidance, asking questions and listening intently to anyone who can help him. At that point in his work life, his job satisfaction is at its peak.

But once he masters his job, it loses its freshness. His duties become routine, and he has fewer learning opportunities. The challenge and variety of his job lessen, hence that initial enthusiasm and commitment. His job goes stale and so does he.

As a manager, you must be alert to this developing problem as it can be a continuing source of subordinate frustration. By searching for ways to renew jobs you can help faltering subordinates restore their job satisfaction, thus their effectiveness and productivity.

ATTITUDES TOWARD STALENESS

The probability that you'll succeed in renewing jobs and revitalizing stale subordinates depends on how aware and concerned they are about what's happening to them. Do they know they have become stale? Are they ignoring it deliberately? Is it causing them any discomfort? Do they know the consequences of their impaired vigor and effectiveness?

Aware and Unconcerned

The subordinate who knows he's stale and doesn't care about it presents your greatest management problem. For example, Pete is a patent attorney for a large corporation. He graduated in the top 10 percent of his law school class. Because of his excellent scholastic record, he was recruited by a leading company.

Initially, he had an opportunity to practice many aspects of corporate law. He was given varied assignments which he performed well. So when one of the senior members of his department left the corporation for another job, he replaced him. Naturally, he was excited about the new job because he was interested in patent law. He learned rapidly and within a year was outperforming his predecessor. That was five years ago, and he's still in the same job. His manager wouldn't think of transferring or promoting him because he relies on his specialized knowledge. To keep him happy, he has given him large salary increases and all the concomitant symbols of success — a company car, a large office decorated tastefully with French provincial furniture, and many perquisites.

Pete's nonpromotable! Unless he decides to leave the company voluntarily, he'll stay in his present job enjoying increasing material rewards but decreasing psychological rewards. Unfortunately, he has become bored and, by his own admission, no longer works at full capacity. He knows he has a problem that will worsen as he gets older. Even though his performance is now highly regarded by his management, he knows he's going stale. But it's not disturbing enough for him to do anything about it.

Because his job had become less challenging, he sought stimulating outside interests. He became a member of the local Republican party and managed the reelection campaign of the local mayor. Attending meetings, giving speeches, and coordinating volunteer activities provided the stimulation he wasn't getting from his job. After helping his candidate to win, he remained active in politics, participating in state-level electioneering. He now spends much of his free time and some work time on this activity.

Perhaps one of your subordinates may also be in the process of winding down and going stale. Yet, he too doesn't do anything about it. He is probably suffering from inertia—a body at rest stays at rest.

Because he's slowed down, it will take a strong personal effort to stop the process and an extraordinary effort to reverse it. But he doesn't need to make that effort because he feels the consequences of being stale or hackneyed are tolerable. Like Pete, the successful corporate lawyer, he may enjoy an excellent salary; he also knows that you like him. And although he's working far below his capacity, nobody's complaining because the changes in his work behavior have occurred gradually. You may overlook them because you're influenced by his outstanding past record and prefer not to change your opinion of him.

Another reason your subordinate may accept his humdrum position is he feels safe. He knows he can work below his capacity indefinitely as long as he fulfills your modest demands and expectations. And to do so, he may be able to lean heavily on others. This is the case for a senior salesman in a major pharmaceuticals company who works in a large metropolitan territory. Nine other salesmen share responsibilities with him for sales in that territory making it virtually impossible to isolate his individual performance. Because of his seniority and ability to impress his manager and others, he is considered an outstanding performer. Yet, for many years, he has not worked hard.

Like Pete, he's unconcerned about lack of stimulation at work because he has found satisfactory substitutes in nonwork activities. By becoming active in a fraternal organization he can win the recognition and status he doesn't get from work. Or, to satisfy his needs, he may become a champion bridge player, a low handicap golfer, a 200+ bowler, or an avid collector or hobbyist. Whatever is missing at work he searches for elsewhere.

This is a healthy process because it helps him cope with his job dissatisfaction. However, it becomes unhealthy when an imbalance develops between work and nonwork. At work, he may develop a short span of attention as his mind wanders to off-the-job plans. He may spend an increasing part of each work day talking to colleagues about his nonwork activities, wasting his time and theirs. As one associate put it:

> Every time I see Steve coming, I run the other way. He never stops talking about his golf game. I think he must spend most of his day wandering from office to office bragging about his last round of golf. And when the weather's nice, I know it's useless to call his office after 3:00. His secretary tells you he's out of the office or had an appointment, but I know where he went.

There are instances in which your subordinate goes stale deliberately. He's angry because he hasn't been promoted and is jealous of those who get opportunities he thinks he deserves. His way of getting even with the company is to slow down to half-speed. He reasons, if you won't give him full recognition, he won't give you a full day's work. Ironically, sometimes he has to work harder trying to avoid work than he would if he were working normally. For example, Beth used to be a highly efficient administrative assistant to a buyer in a large department store. She became upset when one of the other administrative assistants was appointed assistant buyer. Since that time, she has learned to drag her feet on assignments and is generally uncooperative. She's not obvious about what she's doing because she doesn't want to lose her job, but she's definitely much less effective than she was in the past. Although she may feel she's hurting you and the company, she's also hurting herself because her skills will deteriorate from disuse.

Aware and Concerned

Even if your subordinate is aware of and concerned about his staleness, he may be unable to help himself. He has a desire to learn and grow, but has few opportunities to do so. He wants to be creative and innovative, but he can't get you to listen to his ideas. His work standards may be high, but no one seems to appreciate them. And although he knows his job isn't fulfilling and wants to do something about it, he doesn't know how to go about it. You can help him. All he needs is direction from you as to how to revitalize his job.

Totally Unaware

Thus far I've described nonpromotables who know they're stale and who may or may not be concerned about the problem. Many don't know it or choose to ignore it. These people are in trouble because they certainly can't do anything about a problem they don't recognize.

Your subordinate may be unaware of what's happening to him because he refuses to see it—he's afraid to. He doesn't want to concede that he's losing competence. For example, a veteran engineer for a large hard goods manufacturer felt uncomfortable with the new, young engineers. They discussed technology he knew nothing about and found solutions to problems that baffled him. He was disturbed, but did nothing about it because he was afraid to admit to himself that he had allowed himself to become outdated.

Sometimes your subordinate is unaware simply because he lacks introspection. He doesn't know how to step back and take a good, hard look at himself. He doesn't realize he's repeating past mistakes and is surprised when you criticize his performance. He may feel that as long as he tries, whatever he accomplishes will be considered satisfactory. Perhaps you contributed to this attitude by setting low standards in the past; a subordinate has no reason to challenge himself if you appear to be satisfied with his performance.

CAUSES of JOB STALENESS

Time. A major cause of job staleness involves the element of time. The more years a subordinate spends in the same job, the more likely it is to become monotonous. This is particularly true if he works at a job in which there have been minimal changes over the years. He performs the same tasks, works at the same tempo, and with the same people. Thus everything becomes routine and can be performed effortlessly. It ceases to hold his attention.

Lack of Responsibility. Another factor is that your subordinate may not feel responsible for his work. If he's directly accountable for few tasks and can't point to any with pride and say, "I did that!" he begins to feel that it doesn't matter whether he performs well or poorly. Naturally, he's only minimally involved with his job.

Busyness. Paradoxically, another reason a job may become wearisome is busyness. A subordinate's job may have expanded horizontally—the work load has increased, but it's more of the same thing he has been doing all along. He doesn't have the time to think, to innovate, to experiment, or attempt other more challenging tasks.

Restricted Interactions. Perhaps a subordinate works alone or with a limited number of relatively uninteresting people. This situation prevents him from getting a chance to have satisfying learning experiences and expand his views. Also, if the people with whom he interacts are stale themselves, he'll be infected by their jaded attitude.

Narrow Boundaries. You may make a subordinate's job go stale by viewing it narrowly. You set low standards and have low expectations. You don't want your subordinate to trespass outside the narrow boundaries of his job description. You don't care if he possesses greater capabilities than he needs to do the job. Nor do you want to develop his talents so his current job can be expanded.

Motivating Factors. Incentive associated with a job may lose potency. For example, in the past, a subordinate may have had strong drives for money and power. If his current job has satisfied these drives, not completely but sufficiently to push them somewhat into the background, his job becomes less motivating. To maintain incentive, the job would now have to satisfy a new set of higher-order needs.

Unreinforced Good Behavior. A final reason a job may go stale is lack of positive reinforcement for a job well done. You don't reward your subordinate for doing the right things, so there's no reason for him to work hard or try to improve his performance.

JOB ENRICHMENT

You can help your subordinates avoid personal and job staleness. To do so, you must be willing to pay more attention to them, take a genuine interest in them, and try to understand them better. What are their concerns? What are their individual needs and wants? What makes them happy both on and off the job? Are they fully committed to their jobs? Do they feel they are learning and growing? Do they feel you listen to their ideas?

After several years in the same job, your subordinate may feel that his job is unimportant. He wants to take more pride in his personal contribution and wants you and others to recognize his contribution as valuable.

Isn't the answer to his problem simple? If he wants his job to be more important, all you have to do is give him more important things to do. But there's a Catch-22. What you believe to be important may not be important to him; and what he believes to be important may not be important to you. Obviously, agreement on important tasks depends on a reconciliation of your joint opinions. Together you should brainstorm, asking yourselves:

What do we believe needs changing?
What new tasks should be assigned?
How will these new tasks help the company?
Will these tasks be important in the long term as well as the short term?
What priorities should we establish?

In order to add new, important tasks to his work load, your subordinate has to make time available by analyzing his work day. He performs several categories of work activity—automatic, prescribed, selected, and dropped-on-his-desk. The *automatic* activities "come with the job." These are the numerous details that fall under the brief headings that appear in his job description.

Prescribed activities are the special assignments that have been assigned to him either by you or by other members of management. Some of these projects are of short duration; others are ongoing, time-consuming activities.

Selected activities are those he has chosen to do himself. He may make the choice because he likes doing something without thinking about its importance. By so doing, he can destroy the level of importance of his job by choosing to do too many things that are of no consequence to the company.

Dropped-on-his-desk assignments may also make his job

less important. These projects range from small favors for friends, to answering requests for information, to nuisance jobs that associates have persuaded him to do. These activities have a tendency to multiply and consume his work day.

Thus, your subordinate's work load consists of both voluntary and involuntary activities. He can save some time by searching for ways to compress the involuntary activities, asking himself:

Can I use faster, more efficient methods?
Do I have to do all the assignments by myself, or can I delegate to others?
Are all of my involuntary assignments necessary?
How can I eliminate some of them?

Much of the time a subordinate needs to make his job more important is probably available within the area of his voluntary assignments. It's surprising how much time he can save by caring more about what he's doing. And the precious time he saves can be used for more important work.

A Usable System

Ask your subordinates to take a three-dimensional view of their jobs by analyzing activities they like and dislike, activities they do well and don't do well, and activities that they think are important and unimportant. By considering different combinations of these three job dimensions and developing corresponding time strategies, they can make their job more important. Let's look at the effectiveness with which this system can work.

Like, Do Well, Important. Your subordinate may like some aspects of his job because they're interesting and satisfying and he can do them well. Furthermore, if these activities are important, they deserve as much time as he can spare. For example, Natalie is an outstanding writer. Prior to becoming a product marketer she worked as a copywriter in an advertising agency. Although she enjoys her new job, she hasn't lost her love for writing. So, in her present work assignment, she works closely with the creative staff of the advertising agency. Although some of the less talented product marketers in her company tend to let the agency "do the job they're paid to do," she feels it could do a better job with her help. She has a better understanding of the products and the market and has more time to worry about them. She knows that her collaboration with the agency copywriters will produce superior advertisements. So she chooses to spend time on this activity. The benefit to the company has been measurable. Since she joined it, the company's advertising campaigns have been outstanding and the response to them has been unprecedented growth rates.

Like, Don't Do Well, Important. Your subordinate is more apt to complete important assignments that he likes to do. However, if he doesn't do them well, he shouldn't undertake them. He should either first upgrade his skills in order to do them well or get others to help him. For example, Ken doesn't have an aptitude for numbers. He has taken courses in accounting, statistics, and finance to improve his skills, but he still has deficiencies. To compensate for his shortcomings, he relies on well-selected reserves—a secretary who's a whiz at numbers and a friendly divisional controller. Very few of his peers, and none of his superiors, suspect that his numerical skills are weak. He doesn't have to avoid important assignments because he knows where to get the help he needs.

Like, Do Well, Unimportant. The surest way your subordinate can make his job less important is to spend his time doing assignments he likes but which aren't important. The fact that he does them well is meaningless. It's not enough to do things right—instead he should do the right things. For example, Alan spent nearly ten years as a draftsman before becoming an engineer. There is no doubt that he's an expert draftsman. But in his new position he wasted his time double-checking the work of the draftsmen working for him. He often reworked projects that would have been left untouched by other engineers. By spending time on this activity, he made his own job less important. Realizing what he was doing, he changed his focus from "doing" to "managing," and explained to the draftsmen how to improve the quality of their work. Once he knew what was expected of him, Alan learned to trust their performance. This, in turn, freed up the time he had previously spent double-checking their work, and permitted him to concentrate his own efforts on engineering.

Like, Don't Do Well, Unimportant. It's utter foolishness for your subordinate to do unimportant things he doesn't do well. For example, Calvin liked to rewrite contracts. Although he never had any formal legal experience it gave him kicks. It certainly was not expected of him. Unfortunately, when he got through with a contract it was a mess. The company lawyers exchanged jokes about him behind his back. When Calvin learned that these jokes were filtering up to management and were becoming cause for concern, he resolved not to rewrite contracts any more. Instead, he passed suggestions along to the legal staff either by phone or in face-to-face discussions. As long as he allowed them to rewrite the contracts, they welcomed his interest and opinions. And handling contracts in this way saved him time.

Dislike, Do Well, Important. There are assignments that deserve attention. And fortunately your subordinate does them well. But because he dislikes doing them, he tends to put them off, rush them, or do them halfheartedly. Therefore, even though he's capable of doing them well, he performs below his capabilities. To make his job more important, he must give these projects the attention they deserve. Suggest that he try scheduling projects he doesn't like before projects he prefers. This gives him something to look forward to — a reward for completing an unpleasant task. Or, if he has the time, he might divide unpleasant tasks into parts to be done on different days. In this way, he won't have to spend too much of any day doing things he doesn't like to do.

Perhaps the best way to deal with projects he doesn't like is to use his imagination to make them more enjoyable. For example, Dan dislikes making store checks. Every branch manager in his company is required to get into the field regularly to observe store displays, check inventories, and talk with store personnel about competitive activity. To make these field trips more enjoyable, he tries to do more in each store than just talk business. Instead, he has tried to get to know the store personnel. This has double benefits — first, he feels he's visiting old friends instead of strangers, and second, because of the rapport he's developed, they're more cooperative and volunteer valuable information.

Dislike, Don't Do Well, Important. This is one of the most deadly combinations. Such assignments are often pushed aside and forgotten deliberately. Instead, you might show your subordinate how to make them more palatable and help him to get them done well. For example, Len dislikes dealing with the research and development group. He doesn't have the technical background to work comfortably with them. His contacts with research and development personnel usually end up unsatisfactorily. Yet, he recognizes the importance of keeping in close contact with them. His manager suggested that he recruit help from someone in the department. Taking his advice, Len became friendly with one of the chemists, who agreed to supply informal interpretations of anything he didn't understand. By dealing with the problem head-on instead of ignoring it, Len had found a workable solution.

Dislike, Do Well, Unimportant. Sometimes your subordinates get trapped into these kinds of assignments. Colleagues take advantage of the fact that they do them well and ask for help. These individuals should be trained to resist such requests. For example, Ben spent several years as a production foreman. In that job he became proficient at trouble-shooting. Because of this background, he had become the production expert in his department. His colleagues should complain directly to the production foreman when problems arise, but they prefer to ask him to intervene for them. Even though he dislikes doing this, he wants to be a nice guy and is flattered that his colleagues respect his abilities. So he assumes the extra work load, which detracts from more important assignments that he should be doing.

Dislike, Don't Do Well, Unimportant. Your subordinates should spend as little time as possible at these tasks. Yet, inadvertently, if they were to study their work habits they would find that they waste more time on tasks in this category than they think.

The Daily Work Record

The daily work record (Figure 3) will help your subordinates to maintain a record of their daily activities for subsequent analysis.

They should indicate which activities they like or dislike; do well or don't do well; consider important or unimportant. This summary will provide them with a composite picture of how they're spending their time. It helps them answer questions such as: Am I spending too much of my day on assignments I like? In so doing, am I wasting time on unimportant projects and neglecting important projects? Or am I spending too much time on projects I dislike, affecting my performance adversely? How much time am I spending on projects I do well? How much time am I spending on projects I don't do well? Am I spending too little time on important projects? Am I spending too much time on unimportant projects?

FIGURE 3
Daily work record.

TIME	ACTIVITY	LIKE/ DISLIKE	DO WELL/ DON'T DO WELL	IMPORTANT/ UNIMPORTANT
9:00	Reviewed contract	Like	Do well	Important
9:30	Conducted meeting	Dislike	Do well	Unimportant
5:00	Coordinated with R&D	Like	Don't do well	Important
Total		3 hr, Like 4 hr, Dislike	2 hr, Do well 5 hr, Don't do well	3 hr, Important 4 hr, Unimportant

Anyone can make his job more important. All it requires is a plan to increase the number of important assignments he undertakes. He won't have to work any harder because he'll be using his time more wisely. Even when his work load includes a large proportion of assignments which are automatic or prescribed, it's possible to find time for new, important assignments. And everyone has discretionary assignments that should be eliminated, thereby releasing time for more profitable use.

JOB-REDESIGN DISCUSSIONS

Hopefully, the daily work record analysis will convince both you and your subordinates that it pays to maintain a continuing dialog, searching for ways to make jobs more meaningful. Progressive companies have experimented with many techniques to enrich jobs. The following simulated subordinate–superior dialogs describe these techniques and their application in typical work situations.

DISCRETION

Set own goals	Freedom of action
Self-scheduling	Results orientation
Self-control	Open-end assignments
Set own priorities	

Subordinate: You asked me why I'm so dissatisfied with my job. I'll give you an answer you may not like. After fifteen years with this company, I'm tired of being told what to do all the time.

Manager: You feel that you're controlled too tightly?

Subordinate: Yes! I know my job well enough to know what has to be done without having someone look over my shoulder.

Manager: I agree with you. You know your job well. I'm open to any suggestions you might have to redesign your job to give you greater freedom of action. What changes would you like to make?

After a long discussion, both subordinate and manager come to certain conclusions.

Manager: You feel that once I tell you what results the company expects from our department and I expect from you, it's your responsibility to decide how to produce those results?

Subordinate: That's exactly how I feel. I want to set my own work goals, making certain that they don't conflict with either your goals or the company's. I'll work out my schedules and set my own priorities.

Manager: You feel you want to control your own activities as long as you produce results. That sounds reasonable, as long as we can develop a reporting system that will tell us both how well you're doing. I won't interfere unless it becomes obvious that you're not taking necessary corrective action when things go wrong. Of course, I'll be available to provide any assistance you might want.

VARIETY

Assignment rotation	Open-end assignments
Travel	Difficult assignments
Temporary assignments	Work simplification

Subordinate: I'm bored! I get tired of doing the same thing day in and day out.

Manager: You feel that many of the things you do are repetitive and routine. What kinds of assignments would make your job more stimulating and challenging?

Subordinate: I'd like a chance to work with different people, particularly in the field. And I'd like to unload some of my nuisance jobs so I can take on tougher assignments.

Manager: Tell me more about the nuisance jobs you want to unload.

Subordinate and manager engage in an open discussion to examine routine activities and determine which ones can be eliminated and those that are essential.

Manager: We've simplified your job by eliminating some unnecessary routine. Obviously, we can't eliminate all repetitive tasks.

Subordinate and manager then work out ways to vary assignments and to provide greater interaction with other people in the company.

Manager: There are several major problems that our department faces. Suppose I let you try to solve them either individually or as a member of a project team.

Subordinate: I promise you I would give you my full efforts to try to solve those problems.

Manager: Also, you can represent me in selected meetings at branch offices, with our suppliers and customers. In that way, it will relieve me of some of my travel burden and at the same time accomplish your objectives. What else can I do?

Subordinate: Some of the assignments that our staff people handle I would like to do. For example, I feel I could do a really good job of recruiting new people. And I know I could be useful as a trainer.

Manager: You feel you want these special assignments occasionally, not replacing our staff people, but supplementing their efforts?

Subordinate: That's right. I'm not asking for a new job, and I don't want to put anybody else out of a job. But I want new experiences now and then.

RESPONSIBILITY

Whole units of work	High standards
Participation	Increased problem solving
Responsibility for others	Increased decision making

Subordinate: I would like to be in full charge of something. Everybody else gets into the act on all the things I work on. It's hard for me to identify my own contribution.

Manager: You feel you want to be fully accountable, doing your total job by yourself?

Subordinate: I know I can't do my total job by myself. In fact, I really like to work with other people. But I would like to do some things all by myself.

Working together, subordinate and manager identify whole units of work. For example, they agreed he might prepare a total report instead of only contributing to parts of it.

Subordinate: Another thing I don't like is the feeling that I'm a flunky.

Manager: You feel you do menial work?

Subordinate: No. I do many important things. But I would like more of an opportunity to solve my own problems and make my own decisions, or at least to participate more actively.

Manager: What kinds of problems and decisions do you want to have more responsibility for?

The manager works with his subordinate to help him identify areas in which he feels he can be involved in a more meaningful way.

Subordinate: Since I am a senior man in this department, shouldn't I carry more weight than some of the newer men?

Manager: Greater weight? Tell me what you mean by that.

Subordinate: I believe I can help some of the other less experienced men with their jobs. When you're not available, many of them often come to me to ask for advice informally.

Manager: Let's decide specifically where and how you might be able to help them and then discuss it with the men involved. If everybody agrees, let's make the changes.

GROWTH

New learning	High expectations
Experimentation	Developmental opportunities
Career paths	Increased interaction

Manager: You don't seem to be as interested in your job as you used to be.

Subordinate: Maybe I've just been in too long a time. Frankly, I've been thinking about asking for a transfer or quitting.

Manager: Am I contributing to your problem in any way?

Subordinate: No. I just feel I'm not growing. I'm not learning anything and I don't get a chance to do anything different.

Manager: Perhaps we can build some new learning experiences into your current job. Can you think of anything we might try?

Subordinate: Perhaps you could arrange for me to work more closely with someone (within the company or outside the company) from whom I could learn.

The manager reviews with his subordinate different kinds of activities that will help him to feel he's continuing to develop his talents. As the discussion continues, the manager realizes he has been expecting too little from his subordinate. By increasing his demands on him, he actually adds to his satisfaction because he stimulates him to learn and develop.

RECOGNITION

Feedback	Fair appraisals
Special compensation	Career paths
Status symbols	Opportunity to feel important

Manager: You haven't been performing as well recently as you have in the past. Are you having any special problems?

Subordinate: I'm doing as good a job as anybody else. Maybe I have let down somewhat because it doesn't seem to make any difference if I outperform other fellows.

Manager: Do you feel you're not getting sufficient recognition for your efforts?

Subordinate: Except for my annual appraisal in which you pat me on the back and tell me to keep up the good work, I don't feel you do anything special for me.

Manager: Let's discuss what you feel I should have done that I haven't.

The manager explores his subordinate's perceived inequities, and realizes he feels he's been taken for granted.

Manager: Evidently I've been assuming that you knew what I thought about your performance. From what you've been telling me, you'd prefer that I tell you regularly exactly how I feel you are doing — both positive and negative feelings. How else can I help you?

Subordinate: Don't you think I should get special rewards for special accomplishments?

Manager: Let's define what you feel are special accomplishments, and then we can decide what kinds of rewards — monetary and otherwise — might be appropriate.

Working within the constraints of his existing budget, the manager searches with his subordinate for ways to reward mutually agreed-on special accomplishments. During this discussion, the manager is surprised to learn that sometimes relatively inexpensive symbolic rewards serve as well as monetary rewards. For example, a plaque or trophy appears to have significant value to his subordinate.

Manager: Besides the things we've discussed, what else would help you to feel more satisfied?

Subordinate: Well, I know why I haven't been promoted. And I realize my chances for promotion in the future are not very good. But it's hard for me to sit back and watch others advancing.

Manager: You feel you have nothing to look forward to?

Subordinate: That's right! Not only do I feel I'm not going anywhere, but I feel less important because I've been shelved.

Manager: Perhaps by designing a special career path for you we can recognize your contribution and give you a vote of confidence.

Subordinate: Do you mean promotions?

Manager: Not promotion in the traditional sense of moving into completely different responsibilities. Instead, we could add responsibilities to your job and acknowledge them by changing the designation of your job. For example, if in addition to your regular activities as a salesman, we could recognize formally that you are asked to break in new salesmen and call on key customers, it would be appropriate to designate you as a senior salesman. Naturally, additional compensation and perquisites would be associated with that change in status.

For the purpose of illustration, both subordinate and manager are completely open with one another in these dialogs. Actually, when you initiate job-redesign discussions, you may find that your own subordinates are less frank. You'll have to establish rapport and trust to encourage them to confide in you. You will have to be willing to share their career problems with them. That means you'll need to empathize with and penetrate their inner worlds to understand how they feel. You do that by checking continually for understanding, as the manager did in the simulated dialogs: "You feel . . . " "Tell me more . . . " "What do you think . . . ."

As author Clair Vough said in his book *Tapping the Human Resource,*＊ "Human beings have enormous capacity to endure boredom and repetition. Yet, year after year of sustained boredom inevitably leads to staleness." You have to preserve the freshness of your subordinates and the jobs they hold. Your role is that of a facilitator, helping subordinates achieve greater awareness of what's happening to them. Your guidance and cooperation are essential to help make their jobs more important to both themselves and the company. Job renewal is a meaningful alternative to promotion.

＊Clair F. Vough and Bernard Asbell, *Tapping the Human Resource: A Strategy for Productivity* (New York: AMACOM, 1975).

CHAPTER FIVE

Creating
a Motivating Environment

BEHAVIORAL PROBLEMS

Denied advancement and its accompanying rewards, the behavior of many nonpromotables changes, which indicates the onset of motivational problems. I call these predictable behavioral changes the woes — winding down, withdrawing, wandering, wailing, warring, and worrying.

Winding down is manifested by a loss of initiative as well as an avoidance of responsibility. The subordinate who is winding down is careful about "giving away anything for nothing." He feels, "Now that I'm getting less from my job, I'll give less in return."

Subordinates who are *withdrawing* behave like spectators. They're not personally involved with their jobs nor are they committed to the company's objectives. They're disinterested onlookers and indifferent performers.

The behavior of a *wandering* subordinate can be mystifying. That's because he has undergone a basic shift in his work attitudes. Work used to be the primary interest in his life; now it's a weak secondary interest.

Wailing can be one of the most annoying behavioral changes. Previously easy-to-manage subordinates become complainers, grieving about perceived inequities, many of which are petty and imagined.

Warring is manifested by two different kinds of behavioral change. The first is general uncooperativeness and questioning of authority. The second is agitation against you and the company. Either he declares war as an individual or as a member of a clique.

Worrying is a behavioral characteristic that many nonpromotables develop as a result of persistent feelings of insecurity and neglect. They're worried about their present situation and see their futures as grim.

DEFINING the MOTIVATING ENVIRONMENT

The woes cannot thrive in a motivating environment. These self-destructive behavioral changes require the presence of demotivating influences.

Unfortunately, the task of creating a motivating environment is complex because of five major considerations.

1. A motivating environment, according to psychologist Saul Gellerman, "is defined subjectively." It's not the same for everybody. What's motivating for one person may not be motivating for another. For example, you may have a subordinate who has a strong need for achievement; in another this need is weak. Giving demanding assignments to these two subordinates would tend to motivate the first man and demotivate the other.

2. Individual and company needs may conflict. You may not be able to satisfy a subordinate's needs because their fulfillment would be harmful to the company. For example, your subordinate may have a strong need for recognition. Because of that need, he demands more attention than you should reasonably give.

3. A motivating environment is dynamic. Past incentives probably won't continue in the future. As psychologist Abraham Maslow stated in his theory of motivation, when needs are satisfied, "new [and still higher] needs emerge."* For example, give a long-term contract to a man who has a need for security and that need loses its potency as a motivator.

---

*Abraham H. Maslow, *Motivation and Personality,* 2d ed. (New York: Harper & Row, 1970), p. 24.

4. A motivating environment has to satisfy many different needs at the same time. Depending on who's doing the classifying, there's quite an imposing list of needs that serve to motivate people, among which are needs for achievement, affiliation, autonomy, dominance, exhibition, understanding, aggression, esteem, and order.

5. A motivating environment is dependent on achieving a balance between what one gives and one gets. It's a world of trade-offs. Subordinates must be willing and able to change in order to get something they want. For example, a subordinate may have a strong need for esteem, which you help satisfy by increasing his responsibilities. But these new responsibilities force him to reduce the amount of time he spends with close office friends, which interferes with his need for affiliation.

SUBORDINATE–SUPERIOR CONTRIBUTION to a MOTIVATING ENVIRONMENT

A manager who enjoys a strong relationship with a nonpromotable subordinate can help create a work environment motivating enough to neutralize demotivating influences. That's why it's critical that you examine your relationship with any subordinate who appears to be undergoing undesirable behavioral changes. To help you, I have developed the diagnostic instrument shown in Worksheet 5. It is designed to help you surface your attitudes about the subordinate–superior relationship. First work rapidly, giving your top-of-the-head responses. Then put it aside, and a few days later review and challenge your answers. Ask yourself, "Do my responses really reflect my attitudes? What have I done recently that supports or refutes my responses? Will my subordinates concur with my responses?"

Rate each factor as to the extent you feel it provides incentive for a particular subordinate, as well as to what extent you satisfy his needs. For example, for the factor "similarity in work values, " is it very motivating, somewhat motivating, or not motivating to your subordinate? And, do you completely satisfy, somewhat satisfy, or not satisfy his motivational needs?

WORKSHEET 5
Subordinate-superior relationship.

Name _____   Date _____

Characteristics	Motivation Strength			Needs Satisfaction			
	Very Important	Somewhat Important	Not Important	Completely Satisfied	Somewhat Satisfied	Not Satisfied	Does Not Apply
Similarity in work values	☐	☐	☐	☐	☐	☐	☐
Mutual respect	☐	☐	☐	☐	☐	☐	☐
Interdependence	☐	☐	☐	☐	☐	☐	☐
Openness	☐	☐	☐	☐	☐	☐	☐
Shared goals	☐	☐	☐	☐	☐	☐	☐
Cooperativeness	☐	☐	☐	☐	☐	☐	☐
Agreeableness	☐	☐	☐	☐	☐	☐	☐
Understanding	☐	☐	☐	☐	☐	☐	☐
Caring	☐	☐	☐	☐	☐	☐	☐
Helping	☐	☐	☐	☐	☐	☐	☐

Genuineness	☐	☐	☐	☐	☐
Fairness	☐	☐	☐	☐	☐
Consistency	☐	☐	☐	☐	☐
Accessibility	☐	☐	☐	☐	☐
Consideration	☐	☐	☐	☐	☐
Tolerance	☐	☐	☐	☐	☐
Loyalty	☐	☐	☐	☐	☐
Trust	☐	☐	☐	☐	☐
Concreteness	☐	☐	☐	☐	☐
Flexibility	☐	☐	☐	☐	☐

Let's see how you would use this instrument, assuming you have a fictitious subordinate named Tom.

Similarity in Work Values. This is a very important motivational factor for Tom. He likes to feel you have similar values. He values achievement, order, friendship, knowledge, creativity, change and variety, independence, power, and authority.

You believe that you have somewhat satisfied his need for similarity in work values. In many ways you have shown that you value achievement, order, friendship, knowledge, and creativity. But you don't feel that you and Tom share similar values on change and variety, independence, power, and authority. You know Tom would like greater control of his work activities and influence over other people. He has also expressed a desire to make more decisions on his own with less direction from you. And he wants more important work responsibilities. He would also like greater work variety.

Mutual Respect. This factor, you believe, is only somewhat important to Tom. He has a strong self-image and high self-esteem. He doesn't appear to need daily evidence that you respect him, nor does he require a supervisor whom he idolizes.

You feel that you have completely satisfied his needs for mutual respect. You have shown that you value him and his opinions, and have set a reasonably good example so that he has respect for you.

However, this factor could become demotivating if a subordinate has a strong need for mutual respect and perceives that he's disrespected or doesn't have a supervisor he can respect, or both.

Interdependence. Tom tends to be very independent. He doesn't feel he needs your help. Regardless of his independence, he does expect you to support him in many ways; and you depend on him to perform his job well. You rate interdependence as somewhat important to Tom and believe you completely satisfy his needs in this area.

Openness. Tom is a close-mouthed individual. He doesn't confide in you and doesn't expect you to confide in him. Therefore, this is not an important motivating factor for him. And, need satisfaction does not apply.

Shared Goals. Although he is an individualist, Tom expects you to share his personal goals. This is a very important motivating factor for him. However, as you have had disagreements with him about some of his goals, such as his desire for "big money" and advancement, you feel you have not satisfied this need.

Cooperativeness. Tom is a strongly competitive person who continually competes with everybody. Therefore, you rate cooperativeness as not important to him, and need satisfaction does not apply.

Agreeableness. Despite the fact that he's competitive, he doesn't want to alienate you or anybody else. He would prefer to operate within at least a facade of agreeableness, so you rate this factor somewhat important to him. And you feel you completely satisfy his needs, as you are generally agreeable in your relationship with him.

Understanding. Because he is independent, secretive, and competitive, understanding is only somewhat important to him. He doesn't want you to misunderstand him; but he doesn't have a strong need for you to understand him or he would be more open with you. You rate this factor somewhat important.

Because you have been unable to establish a feeling of closeness with Tom, you believe you have only somewhat satisfied even his modest need for understanding. That's because he has resisted your attempts to get to know him.

Caring. This factor is somewhat important to Tom. Because he is an individualist, he doesn't want a supervisor who fawns over him, but he does expect you to show you care about him.

You feel you have completely satisfied this need. Regardless of your difficulties in reaching him, you have demonstrated that you're interested and concerned with him.

Helping. Paradoxically, this is a very important motivating factor for Tom. He wants freedom of action and is strongly independent, but he expects you to be supportive and to properly represent him to higher management. Since he has strong expectations in this area, you feel you have not satisfied them. You have tried to be helpful, but that helpfulness has not been perceived as satisfactory to Tom.

Genuineness. This is only somewhat important to Tom. Since he tends to be manipulative, he doesn't expect complete sincerity from you. In fact, he's accustomed to, and likes, a certain amount of game-playing. You completely satisfy his modest needs for genuineness.

Fairness. This is a very important motivator to Tom. He demands fair treatment and is very sensitive to favoritism. Because he knows you feel he is nonpromotable, he believes you favor those who are promotable in his group. Therefore, you do not satisfy his needs.

Consistency. This is another strong motivator for Tom. He expects you to be consistent in your behavior. He likes to predict how you would act in a given situation. Since Tom makes very strong demands in this area, you feel you only somewhat satisfy his needs. You're generally consistent, but not as consistent as Tom would like you to be.

Accessibility. This is not important to Tom. He doesn't require frequent associations with you, nor is it important that you be easy to talk to. Because it is not important to him, need satisfaction does not apply.

Consideration. This is only somewhat important to Tom. He doesn't require special attention, but he doesn't want to be ignored. He certainly doesn't want to be abused. You feel you completely satisfy his needs.

Tolerance. This is a somewhat important factor for Tom. Although he has strong biases and tends to be intolerant, he expects more from you. He wants you to be aware of your own biases and resents being stereotyped in any way. Furthermore, he expects you to be tolerant of any lapses in his performance. Because it's difficult to meet Tom's rigid standards for tolerance, you feel you only somewhat satisfy his needs.

Loyalty. This is not important to Tom. He isn't strongly allegiant to others, and he doesn't expect it in return. Therefore, need satisfaction does not apply.

Trust. This is a very important motivator to Tom. He demands that you trust him implicitly. He wants your full confidence. You believe you're reasonably trustful, but can only somewhat satisfy Tom's strong needs.

Concreteness. This is a very important motivator for Tom.

He would like to live in a black-and-white work world in which roles, expectations, and standards are clearly defined. You feel that in his eyes, you don't satisfy his needs.

Flexibility. This is not important to Tom. He's inflexible and doesn't expect flexibility from others. On the contrary, he admires people who adhere rigidly to positions and considers flexible people to be weak. Since you tend to be a flexible person, and will change your mind when faced with convincing evidence, you don't satisfy Tom's needs in this regard.

In completing an exercise like this one, you spotlight certain aspects of your relationship with a subordinate. You should recognize interrelationships among clusters of motivating factors and realize that need satisfaction is closely related to motivation strength. You may be satisfying needs according to your own standards, but not according to those of your subordinate. To create a motivating environment you must reconcile differences in areas in which you are only somewhat satisfying or not satisfying important motivational factors.

MEASURING a MOTIVATING ENVIRONMENT

After completing the subordinate–superior relationship analysis, you may feel that you know what motivates your subordinate and how well you feel you satisfy his needs. These are your unverified assumptions. You can verify them directly or indirectly.

The *direct approach* is to schedule a counseling interview and simply ask your subordinate about his morale and the factors that contribute to it, particularly those you can influence. With some subordinates, this may yield valuable information and reinforce your assumptions or force you to abandon them. With other subordinates, this method yields sparse and questionable information. Perhaps the subordinate is not introspective and just doesn't know what motivates him. Or he may believe he is influenced by particular motives, when in reality he is substituting one motive for another. For example, many people believe that their strongest motive is money, whereas what they really are motivated by is the status or power it represents.

Sometimes subordinates may be unwilling to tell you their motives because they are embarrassed to admit them. This is particularly true when the subordinate considers a motive to be socially undesirable. For example, few subordinates will admit that they have a strong need to dominate others.

Regardless of the fact that the direct method will probably not provide complete or accurate information, it's worth trying. It demonstrates your interest in your subordinate and gives you a rough indication of how well you understand him.

The *indirect approach* to measuring motives takes more time than the direct approach. You measure motives by searching for congruity — do your own assumptions about a subordinate's motives, his stated opinions about what motivates him, and his behavior appear to be in agreement?

By carefully observing your subordinate's behavior over a period of time, you'll be able to detect recurring patterns which confirm the existence of strong motives. Let's examine five short case histories, each describing recurring behavior patterns, suggesting the existence of a strong underlying motive:

1. Tim is a fifty-two-year-old foreman who supervises a group of ten workmen in a chemical processing operation. His boss considers him to be an ideal employee. He never complains, even when he's doing tasks he obviously doesn't like. He's so cooperative and overly conforming that some of his colleagues consider him a "yes" man. Normally he is agreeable and rarely confronts anybody unless he is forced to. He likes things "the way they are" and doesn't want to do anything new and different because he's fearful of jeopardizing his job. About the only changes he welcomes are those that provide protection for the future, particularly his job continuity. The dominant underlying motive that influences his behavior is security.

2. Sara is one of the most popular women in the personnel department. She's treasurer of the credit union, active in the bowling league, and an organizer of special office social events. She's anxious to please others and prefers to withhold her opinion if it might antagonize anybody. The few people who are her detractors accuse her of "following the crowd." Sara is loyal to friends and is very helpful to them. She's

willing to share things with friends and would rather do things with them than work alone. Her behavior is influenced by a strong affiliation motive.

3. Ed is a difficult person to manage. He's frequently involved in rivalries; he's continually complaining of inequities; he demands special treatment; he boasts of his personal achievements; he wants to feel important and admired by others; and he is forever seeking approval for his actions. The reason Ed behaves as he does is because he responds to a strong need for esteem.

4. Marie likes to be the center of attention. She asks for spotlight assignments, makes sure she gets credit for her accomplishments, tends to dominate meetings, likes to have others notice and comment on her appearance, and likes to say things just to see what effect it will have on others. The strong motive that influences Marie's behavior is recognition.

5. Marvin is an outstanding individual performer but a poor team worker. He competes ruthlessly and is intolerant of colleagues. He seeks his own way and wants to be right. In group situations he tries to take charge. He likes to do difficult jobs well and solve difficult problems. And he delights in being told that he can do things better than others. The same motive that tends to make him effective also causes him considerable grief. He is strongly influenced by a need for achievement.

The value in developing working assumptions about subordinates and trying to verify these assumptions is it gives you standards against which you can measure their behavior. Instead of making casual and random observations, you search for specific behavior patterns. For example, you have a gut feeling that a subordinate has a strong need for recognition. In a counseling interview, you ask him what motivates him and he provides some confirmatory evidence that your assumption about his need for recognition is correct. Thereafter, when you have occasions to observe him in action, you look for manifestations of this need, recording in writing specific events that confirm or disprove your assumption.

Over a period of time, you are able to develop a motivation profile. That profile is invaluable in guiding your relationship with your subordinate. With it you can predict how he is likely to react in different situations.

An accurate motivation profile will help you to recognize, understand, and deal with undesirable behavior that results from unfulfilled needs. You will know from profiling a subordinate that one of the motives that strongly influences him is a need for esteem. You will recognize that many of the problems you are having in managing him are directly related to that need. The more frustrated he becomes in trying to satisfy this need, the more he "acts up" in a struggle to enhance his esteem. By planning changes in his work environment that will satisfy his motivational need, you can get him to change his undesirable behavior.

STRATEGIES for ATTACKING
NEGATIVE BEHAVIOR

Earlier in this chapter I discussed the behavioral changes associated with nonpromotability, which I called the woes. Nonpromotables develop strong negative feelings that influence their behavior because they have been unable to satisfy basic needs. I suggested that if you profile the motivational drives that evoke these feelings and behaviors in your subordinates, you are in a position to plan strategies to counteract them. Figure 4 indicates the positive strategies you can use to create a motivating environment in which negative behaviors and feelings won't survive. Let's see how you can use these strategies to attack the six behavior problems.

Winding Down

Assume that the behavior of one of your subordinates indicates that he is winding down. From discussions with him, you learn that he feels frustrated because his earlier hopes to rise to a level of importance in the company have not been realized. He feels disappointed, perhaps to the point of being depressed. He feels that a door has been slammed in his face and now he's excluded from all the privileges awaiting his promotable colleagues. To counteract his winding down, you might appeal to his unsatisfied needs for responsibility and achievement. You ask yourself, "What new responsibilities should I delegate to him?" and "How can I give him opportunities for personal achievement?"

FIGURE 4
Strategies for creating a motivating environment.

BEHAVIOR	FEELINGS	STRATEGY
Winding down	Frustrated Disappointed Excluded	Responsibility and achievement
Withdrawing	Alienated Neglected Rejected	Psychological closeness and affiliation
Wandering	Bored Indifferent Uncommitted	Involvement and self-control
Wailing	Hurt Unappreciated Envious	Recognition and esteem
Warring	Hostile Vindictive Cheated	Positive interaction and communication
Worrying	Out-of-date Unimportant Intimidated	Growth and learning

Responsibility. As their competence grows, most subordinates expect more responsibilities. Routine tasks are tolerated when interspersed with more demanding assignments. Thus, responsibility can be a motivating strategy. Examine your own job to see if there are duties that can be assigned to your subordinate. Doing this serves a double purpose — it releases you to accept new responsibilities yourself and concentrate on managing as well as satisfying his needs. For example, using forecasting information supplied by your subordinate, you work with the production planning department to develop production schedules. In performing this particular managerial task, you're a middle man. Instead, you could ask your subordinate to deal directly with production planning. By doing so, you add a satisfying new responsibility to his duties and demonstrate your confidence in him.

Achievement. To accomplish something you're proud of, to meaningfully complete a task, and to solve a difficult problem, are all sources of motivation. You can exploit the need to achieve by providing your subordinate with opportunities to isolate his or her own contributions.

For some people, relatively minor accomplishments can provide the joyful feeling of achievement. Others are much more demanding of themselves. When using achievement as a strategy for motivating your subordinate, you must recognize these differences. For instance, one subordinate's need for achievement may be satisfied by assigning him responsibility for developing relatively simple reports, whereas another may require complex, open-ended assignments, such as taking charge of a cost-improvement task force.

Withdrawing

The nonpromotable who shows symptoms of withdrawal feels alienated. In his mind, he has been pushed aside. He tends to magnify feelings that he's being neglected and forgotten. In an effort to cope with these feelings of rejection, he withdraws from those he feels have rejected him. To bring him back and get him to participate actively again, you might use strategies of psychological closeness and affiliation.

Psychological Closeness. Subordinates tend to respond favorably to managers who exhibit warmth, consideration, and a genuine interest. By the way you act toward them, you show that you really care about them as individuals. Some managers who have difficulty in expressing warmth and showing consideration cynically refer to these qualities as "handholding." But they're mistaken; in order to manage subordinates who are wary of rejection you must establish a mutual feeling of psychological closeness.

Affiliation. The need to belong to a friendly, cooperative work team is, to some extent, shared by all of us. People are social beings. They want good interpersonal relationships. They gain strength from each other. But effective work teams are built on interdependence. Yet some supervisors sabotage their own work groups by encouraging rivalries and divisiveness. The supervisor intent on creating a motivating environment should focus on team-building practices and take advantage of member need for identification with the group. For instance, you might assign a withdrawing subordinate to a work project that puts him right in the middle of things, working closely with compatible peers who not only accept him but welcome his participation.

Wandering

The wandering nonpromotable is attracted to nonwork activities because work has become boring to him. He performs his job in a perfunctory way, indifferent to his responsibilities, and uncommitted to you and the company. He feels work is something he has to do, not something he wants to do.

To make his work environment more motivating, you have to ask yourself, "How can I create opportunities for his involvement in problem solving and decision making?" and "How can I exert greater control over how he performs his job?"

Involvement. Given an opportunity to share in problem solving and decision making, subordinates are more apt to identify with organizational objectives and make them their own. By so doing, they become more motivated and committed.

If you're willing to share your responsibilities, there are many times when you could ask for the advice of subordinates, particularly when your decisions affect them personally. By being allowed to participate in problem solving and decision making, they develop greater appreciation for actions you must take. For example, the director of a large research and development group was critical of the uninspired performance of one of his technologists. Yet he knew that the same man invested extraordinary time and effort into nonwork projects. He therefore invited his subordinate to attend weekly brainstorming sessions in his specialty area. At these sessions, group members shared their work problems and solicited help in making decisions. Because there was considerable peer pressure to participate, and the subjects under discussion di-

rectly affected those present, he became actively involved in
the discussions.

Self-control. Placing the burden for control on a subordinate's back can often renew his interest in his job. Knowing
that no one will be looking over his shoulder to spot his mistakes or to tell him he's behind schedule, your subordinate
will find it difficult to be indifferent to his responsibilities.
Self-control can be a powerful motivator, provided your subordinate's performance can be measured effectively and he has
participated in setting the standards of measurement. For instance, a manager in an EDP department was dissatisfied with
the productivity of one of this programmers. He met with him
and negotiated reasonable standards both for quality and
quantity of work. They agreed that he would accept full responsibility for meeting the standards and would develop self-
controls to spot deviations early enough to take corrective action.

Wailing

The wailing nonpromotable is a troubled individual. He
feels hurt because you didn't promote him. Even if he admits
that you were justified, he still feels you let him down. He
feels that you don't appreciate his past loyalty and friendship.
To his mind, he had tried hard and given you full effort, but
that wasn't enough to win your support. Furthermore, he feels
envious of those you did promote because you have shown
that you favor them. To create a more motivating environment,
you have to prove that you recognize his contribution and take
steps to restore his self-esteem.

Recognition. Genuine words of praise for well-deserved
performance can work wonders in motivating someone. In
fact, success makes subordinates feel "ten feet high" and
makes them want to achieve more success. Although your subordinate may feel he did something worthwhile, success is
"sweeter" when important spectators like yourself both
witness and acknowledge it. You can do this by writing a formal letter of commendation with carbon copies to all interested parties, or you can post it on the bulletin board. At the
very least, acknowledge it informally by telling him you're

pleased with his contribution. Don't assume that he already knows you appreciate it.

Esteem. Even the humblest of us enjoys impressing others. When others respect us, we have greater respect for ourselves. In contrast, when others disrespect us, we tend to have less respect for ourselves. Thus, how you relate to your subordinate can be enhancing or damaging to his self-esteem. By being considerate, appreciative, and respectful, you let your subordinate know that you value his services. If you are condescending, arrogant, and aloof, you tell him just the opposite.

Particularly important is how you treat him in front of others. Praise and criticism both have more impact when onlookers are present. By complimenting a subordinate for special accomplishments or thanking him for a special effort, you help build the subordinate's opinion of himself as well as the group's opinion of him.

Warring

Warring nonpromotables are carrying a grudge. They are hostile because they feel mistreated. They'd like to strike back at everybody who has had a hand at bringing their career to a standstill. They feel cheated and deprived of promotions they deserved. To motivate a subordinate in this state of mind, you have to keep lines of communication open and arrange for continuing positive interaction.

Communication. By talking regularly and openly to your subordinate, you can surface the strong, negative feelings that are contributing to his belligerence. He should feel free to ask questions and get honest and direct answers. Don't try to defend your position or convince him of your rightness. Instead, encourage him to clear the air and express his feelings. You can't argue with emotions. Instead, listen patiently to them and accept them. Once his initial anger abates, he'll want to know more about the impact of his nonpromotability on his present and future status. You can help him to develop a realistic, yet optimistic, view of the options open to him.

Positive Interaction. The more frequently you interact with a subordinate in a positive way, the more opportunity you have to dispel his strong negative feelings. You demonstrate by the way you work with him that you trust him, have confidence in him, respect him, genuinely care about him, and want to help him. It's difficult to bear a grudge against someone who acts positively toward you. On the other hand, if you allow a subordinate's negative attitudes to affect you — and you reflect them back — you widen the gap.

Mutual problem-solving situations provide natural opportunities for positive interaction. When you both have the same objectives, your interdependence will tend to bring you together. Other positive interaction opportunities occur naturally in group situations in which you can ally yourself with him and support his points of view.

Worrying

Worrying nonpromotables feel they are losing their competence and becoming obsolete. They're worried because they no longer feel important. They lose their self-confidence and are fearful of further losses in status, responsibility, perhaps even their jobs. One of the most effective ways to help overcome the doubts and insecurities of a nonpromotable subordinate is to develop growth and learning strategies.

Growth. "Realizing one's potential" is a shared responsibility of supervisor and subordinate. Whereas some people grow in spite of their supervisors, most of us can use a boost. Guidance begins with the supervisor's interest and belief in our capacity for growth. It requires his support and encouragement. Contrast these opposing attitudes toward personal growth and consider their impact on subordinates.

All I'm interested in is what my subordinates do today in their current job. If they complete assignments satisfactorily, what else can I expect from them?

I'm committed to the personal development of my subordinates. By helping them to acquire new skills, I increase their satisfaction, productivity, quality of performance, and capacity to assume greater responsibility.

Learning. Learning is valued by those who recognize it as a key to responsibilities, achievement, and growth. It helps your subordinates feel important and confident. Hence, your role as a teacher is important to the job happiness of your subordinates. To the extent that you keep up to date yourself and share your knowledge and experience with subordinates, it contributes to their motivation. You should welcome informal teaching (coaching) relationships with subordinates, and should also schedule, when available, regular formal teaching opportunities within and outside the company. Naturally, teaching shouldn't be force-fed to unwilling subordinates. Instead, it should be directed to and focused on those who want to learn.

Using the motivating strategies discussed, you can create "islands of satisfaction" in even the most demotivating of work environments. Although you have an obligation to work for positive change over the long run, in the total work environment you can begin immediately to "get your own house in order." However, in doing so, remember that no single strategy will suffice, and that not everybody under your supervision will be receptive to all the strategies because people have different needs. Furthermore, not all are ready for higher motivational methods—some like to be dependent, like control and repetitive work, don't want responsibility and advancement. About the only universally motivating forces are: to know what you expect from them, to get fast feedback on how they are doing, and to be recognized and rewarded for doing the right things.

To be an effective supervisor, you should try periodically to determine the state of morale within your work group, understanding the needs of your subordinates and recognizing to what extent your own relationship with them enhances or damages the motivational environment. This is of particular importance in dealing with nonpromotables who are undergoing undesirable behavioral changes because of their nonpromotability. The ultimate payoff for your efforts to create a more motivating environment is a highly productive and satisfied work group.

CHAPTER SIX

The Helping Appraisal

Performance appraisal, as it is currently practiced in most companies, isn't perceived to be helpful by the employee cast in the role of the nonpromotable. As far as this individual is concerned, its primary purpose is to evaluate whether he is performing well enough to keep his current job and earn a nominal salary increase. At these annual events, his manager passes judgment on his personal worth, and he is placed in the uncomfortable position of having to listen to what's wrong with him and the way he performs his job. His manager will probably intersperse criticism with words of praise, but a subordinate under attack (as he views criticism) doesn't listen carefully to whatever praise is uttered and what he does hear has little effect on him.

Supposedly, evaluative aspects of the performance appraisal are secondary to its major purpose, that is, helping a subordinate to improve his performance by "letting him know how he stands." This is intended to contribute to his personal development and motivation. You believe, by pointing out weaknesses, that you are helping him see things in himself and his performance that he overlooks.

There are many reasons why your subordinate, particularly a nonpromotable subordinate, doesn't appreciate this kind of help. The major reason is that your diagnosis often isn't valid. It may be based on insufficient information that he believes

doesn't concern him or isn't representative of his performance. For instance, you may criticize him about how he uses
his time. However, he may have differing views as to his job
requirements and work priorities.

Another reason he may not accept your criticism is that he
doesn't believe you're qualified to give it to him. Perhaps he
feels he has more experience and expertise than you. Or he
may feel that many of his problems are created by you, that his
weaknesses stem from obstacles that you have put in his path.
For example, he is late in meeting deadlines because you
keep piling unimportant assignments on his desk, which
prevents him from performing his primary responsibilities.

Often, he is acutely aware of his weaknesses. In fact, his
previous managers may have pointed out the same weaknesses. And he knows these kept him from getting promoted.
But, unfortunately, they're not remediable, in which case constantly nagging him about his weaknesses doesn't help him at
all. A case in point is a supervisor in a quality control department who has considerable technical expertise. Despite his
high level of competence his managers have been telling him
that he is not "forceful enough." He's a meek man who avoids
confrontation. He knows it and so does everybody who works
with him. He would like to do something about it and has tried
in the past. But he has been unsuccessful because basic personality changes are very difficult, if not impossible, to make.

Sometimes no matter what a subordinate does, he is unable
to please you. You may expect too much from him. Unconsciously, you may want him to be "just like you." But, he's unable to, or doesn't want to, be a carbon copy of you. If you're a
very orderly person, you would probably be intolerant of any
disorderliness in a subordinate. Or if you're an independent
thinker, accustomed to showing strong initiative, it would be
difficult for you to accept a subordinate who tends to be
dependent and won't act unless he checks with you first.

Even if he can live up to your basic requirements, your subordinate may feel that he just can't seem to please you. That's
because you harp on petty faults and give the impression that
these minor deficiencies are as important to you as the performance of major responsibilities. For example, a manager in
a busy order-processing department has a highly effective sub-

ordinate; but he continually criticizes his appearance with the attitude that anyone who doesn't have a neat appearance will give others the impression that his work is disorderly.

One of the major reasons your subordinate may refuse to accept your criticism is that he doesn't feel the reward for correcting what you consider a weakness is worth the effort. Furthermore, what you want him to do may be something he dislikes, which makes it more rewarding not to correct his weaknesses. For example, in his annual appraisals, a manager with ten years in the same job is criticized by his boss as "being too easy" with his subordinates. He realizes that his boss's evaluation is accurate, but finds no incentive to change. He earns the maximum in his salary range, and his annual bonus is a fixed percentage of his gross salary. He also realizes that it's unlikely that he will be promoted, as he has been passed over for promotion several times. By complying with his boss's suggestion, he would disrupt his relationship with his own subordinates. He refuses to change because he enjoys the feeling of being well liked and accepted as "one of the boys."

THE NEGATIVE CONSEQUENCES
of MISHANDLING APPRAISALS

Regardless of your good intentions, the way in which you conduct an appraisal can have negative consequences. A major study conducted by General Electric proved that "defensiveness that results from critical appraisal produces inferior performance."[*] It can also add a strain to the relationship between you and your subordinate. And, of particular importance to the nonpromotable, it serves to lower his self-esteem. It may even be threatening, which makes him fearful about keeping his job, and immobilizes him. This sets in motion a vicious cycle — he doesn't perform well, you criticize him, and he then becomes afraid to do anything he's unsure of because he doesn't want to place his job in greater jeopardy. His re-

[*]Herbert H. Meyer, Emanuel Kay, and John R. P. French, Jr., "Split Roles in Performance Appraisal," *Harvard Business Review*, Jan.–Feb. 1965, p. 124.

fusal to experiment with new things and change his way of operating causes his performance to continue downhill.

These negative consequences are aggravated when a manager mishandles the appraisal interview. Here are ten common pitfalls that may trap you.

1. *The manager in a hurry.* You may feel, as many managers do, that the appraisal interview is a chore and really has no value. You conduct it only because company policy requires it. As a result, you tend to rush it and try to get it over with as quickly as possible. Your subordinate interprets your behavior as a lack of interest in him.

2. *The unprepared manager.* Because you feel it really doesn't count for much, you spend very little time preparing for the appraisal. If you're using the traditional essay form, your comments lack depth — they're brief, too general, and superficial. If you're using the rating-scale-type appraisal, you tend to be careless and arbitrary in your selections, not bothering to gather evidence to support your ratings.

3. *The biased manager.* If you like your subordinate, you rate him highly; if you don't like him, you rate him poorly. Any evidence you present, you've gathered to support your point of view, not to arrive at an accurate appraisal of performance.

4. *The dogmatic manager.* You tell your subordinate how you feel about his performance. You don't want to hear any back talk explaining his deficiencies. You've made your judgments and they're final.

5. *The manipulative manager.* By skillful use of praise and criticism, you expect to manipulate a subordinate into acting as you want him to. You don't consider his personal needs. You're not interested in understanding his point of view or problems. You have decided that you know what's good for him and are determined to talk him into taking specific actions.

6. *The manager who blocks participation.* You don't give your subordinate a say in his appraisal. He's neither given an opportunity to justify his past performance nor to participate in setting goals, determining priorities, and planning the best way to accomplish future objectives. In effect, you tell him that you don't value his opinions.

7. *The manager who gives undue weight to recent events.* LIFO (last in, first out) is a method of accounting that often applies to a manager's appraisal process. Recently, one of your subordinates did something outstanding—either good or bad. When you appraise him, these actions affect your feelings about him and his performance. This is particularly true when his performance failure has caused you personal embarrassment. For example, a programmer with a solid record of performance fouled up on the program for a report that was distributed to virtually all of the management group. As a result of that foul-up, the director of EDP received considerable abuse. Shortly thereafter, when he appraised that programmer, he did so with vengeance, giving him the worst ratings he ever had.

8. *The manager who judges "how" rather than "what."* Even if you and your subordinate agree in advance (and most don't) on standards of performance, you may slant your evaluation because you did not spell out exactly how you wanted him to act in carrying out assignments. Like Zero Mostel in the play *Stop the World, I Want to Get Off,* you keep changing the rules, particularly with regard to the amount of initiative expected from your subordinate. You want him to accomplish a task, but you want him to do it your way.

9. *The manager who makes up his mind prematurely.* Before you listen to your subordinate's explanations or evaluate any facts, you decide you know all about him. You know whether he has performed effectively; you know his deficiencies; you know what he needs to do to improve. You've made up your mind and you don't want any facts to interfere with your judgment. The possibility that deficiencies in a subordinate's job performance may be due to inadequate training, poor supervision, incomplete communication, or low motivation does not occur to you.

10. *The manager who doesn't tell all.* A fascinating study done by Douglas McGregor showed that forty percent of employees in one company with a well-planned and carefully administrated appraisal program indicated they had never had the experience of being told "where they stand." Yet, company files showed that four-fifths of them had signed a form testifying they had been through an appraisal interview, some

of them several times. Obviously, their managers didn't tell all. They deliberately withheld information.

MANAGERIAL REJECTION
of CONVENTIONAL APPRAISALS

You may feel, as many managers do, that you would not conduct appraisal interviews if it were not company policy. You don't see the advantages in doing so, yet you can see many disadvantages. You believe you are continually appraising your subordinates, and you're more concerned with improving their performance in day-to-day coaching situations. In your mind, formal appraisals are unnecessary.

As Douglas McGregor wrote in explaining manager resistance to undertaking conventional appraisals, "Managers are uncomfortable when they are put in the position of 'playing God.' "[*] You're either unwilling or lacking confidence that you can accurately rate subordinates on the many variables listed on traditional appraisal forms. How can you, when most of your subordinates perform in the "nonextreme range" — neither outstandingly good or bad?

Furthermore, you may not want to air your "dirty wash" for the rest of the company to see. For if you criticize a subordinate strongly, and it becomes part of his permanent record, you then put yourself in the position of having onlookers interested in how you handle the situation. You would therefore prefer that it be a private matter between you and your subordinate. Because you feel this way, you might cover up during the formal appraisal so your subordinate doesn't look bad to others, thus reflecting on you.

Assuming, however, that you're not concerned about how others may react to your appraisal reports, you should be concerned what your subordinate will think. If you criticize him, will you face an uncomfortable confrontation? Will he become an adversary? Because the average subordinate tends to rate himself higher than his manager does, unless you rate him "excellent" in all aspects of his performance, you're likely to antagonize him and create bad feelings that could carry over to

[*] Douglas McGregor, *The Human Side of Enterprise* (New York: McGraw-Hill, 1960).

your daily working relations. It's natural to ask yourself, "What do I gain and risk by being completely honest in my appraisals?"

THE HELPING APPRAISAL
vs. the CONVENTIONAL APPRAISAL

In contrast to the conventional appraisal, the helping appraisal shifts emphasis from evaluation to mutual performance planning and future goal-setting. And unlike the conventional appraisal, the helping appraisal is something you do with rather than to subordinates. You don't have to play God, passing judgment on them. You aren't forced to make them adversaries by confronting them about their weaknesses. Nor do you have to complete arbitrary rating scales. Instead, you and your subordinate work together and analyze problems critical to improving his performance. If done properly, it will simplify his management and control.

Your subordinates should be more receptive to helping appraisals than to conventional ones. It will satisfy their need to know where they stand as well as what's expected of them. It will also give them an opportunity to influence their futures by participating in performance planning, goal-setting, and preagreement on the rewards for good performance.

Most importantly, the helping appraisal should create positive feelings rather than the negative attitude associated with conventional appraisals. There's no reason to be apprehensive about them because your subordinates have nothing to lose and everything to gain. They won't have to meet with a judge who will reprimand them for things they've done wrong in the past. Instead, they will be meeting with someone who's vitally interested in truly helping them perform at a level that will protect their job security and give them satisfactory rewards.

The difference between the conventional appraisal and the helping appraisal, as seen through the eyes of the appraisee, is best described by this abstract from an actual interview with someone who had experienced his first helping appraisal.

I was wary, as usual, on entering my boss's office for my annual appraisal. I expected to see his *official* opinions of my year's performance reduced to 1–10 ratings of my productivity, initiative, attitude, abilities, and so forth. I dreaded the one-sided arguments we would have over whether I was a "5" or a "7"; or worse yet, a "2" or a "5." In those confrontations, I always lost because I was seeing the ratings for the first time, and he had an opportunity to gather evidence in advance to support his point of view.

This time it was different. I wasn't on the spot. There weren't any irritating ratings of my past performance. I wasn't a passive spectator. My boss didn't have any preconceived notions. We sat down together with a blank piece of paper to discuss my problems, as seen through my eyes. We worked together to remove obstacles and to arrange for any help I might want.

For the first time, unlike past appraisals, we weren't sitting on opposite sides of the table as adversaries. He was genuinely interested in helping me. That was a great feeling!

ESSENTIALS for the HELPING APPRAISAL

After years of exposure to conventional performance appraisals, both you and your subordinate have probably developed attitudes that would interfere with the helping appraisal. These attitudes have to be put on the table and discussed before you can hope to accomplish anything in a helping appraisal. The following dialog illustrates the content of a typical discussion about attitudes essential to a helping appraisal:

Manager: Our company has had a change in policy regarding performance appraisal procedures. I think the change makes a lot of sense because I'm no longer put in the uncomfortable position of having to tell you what you do right and do wrong.

Subordinate: How can you conduct an appraisal without reviewing my performance?

Manager: We won't ignore the past, but it will be meaningful only in terms of problems you feel might interfere with your future performance.

Subordinate: Suppose I feel I don't have any problems and that my performance will be outstanding in the future without any interference from anybody?

Manager: If you feel that way, my job will be easy. All we'll have to do is share your plans so I know what you're trying to accomplish and agree on standards by which to measure those accomplishments. However, I suspect that there are some areas in which you feel some need for improvement.

Subordinate: But if I ask for help, don't I put myself in the position of spotlighting my own weaknesses?

Manager: I hope so. Because unless you do spotlight them, I'm in no position to offer my own assistance or make available other resources to help you overcome them.

Subordinate: But I don't want to look bad. That will affect my salary increases and your opinion of me.

Manager: From our day-to-day working relations, I have already formed many impressions about you and your performance. Some may be accurate and others inaccurate. Ordinarily, I would make an independent judgment as to how well you're performing based on my own standards. Now, under the new system, we'll work together to decide how your performance will be measured and agree on standards as well as appropriate rewards for accomplishments.

Subordinate: Will I really have an equal voice in planning my performance and setting standards?

Manager: I want you to use your full talents and perform to the best of your ability. I'm willing to do whatever is necessary to assist you in accomplishing these objectives. So you *can't* have an equal voice in your future plans — your feelings and opinions have to have greater weight than mine! You must do the job and I'll provide whatever help I can.

During the subsequent discussion, the manager emphasized the need for reciprocal trust and openness between him and his subordinate. He explained that their mutual growth is linked to the need for feelings of interdependence: "I help you, and you help me." The subordinate must be willing to share his problems and to search with his manager for innovative ways to solve them. They have to learn from each other and be tolerant of differences. And, most importantly, they have to be realistic.

It is difficult to build this kind of rapport during the helping appraisal. Your subordinate is likely to be somewhat fearful and distrustful in being exposed to a new approach. And it will be difficult for you to depart from your usual posture of evaluating and advice-giving. Also, you'll have to overcome your natural tendency to want to steer your subordinate in a particular direction and control the outcome of the appraisal. In the same way, your subordinate will keep testing you to determine whether it's "business as usual," masquerading under a new name.

Your first helping appraisal probably won't go smoothly. Both you and your subordinate are likely to resist the change in procedure, particularly because it will demand much more of both of you than do traditional appraisals. It will require more time, preparation, and in-depth discussion.

THE HELPING APPRAISAL PROCESS

A scheme for the helping appraisal process is shown in Figure 5. Step 1 is the preappraisal discussion. The purpose of this discussion, as I indicated in the previous section, is to establish a favorable climate for the subsequent appraisal. Without a reasonable measure of mutual trust and openness and a willingness to experiment and learn from each other, the helping appraisal shouldn't take place. If you already have good rapport with your subordinate, a single preappraisal discussion might suffice. However, most managers find that bad past experiences with performance appraisals sensitize subordinates to any appraisal situation. Therefore, it may take a series of general discussions of 30 to 45 minutes each to establish a favorable climate. During these discussions, you should explore in an unstructured way your subordinate's attitudes about the company, his job, his general level of satisfaction, and his relationship with you. When you feel that you have reached a point at which you can both talk freely, where you trust one another and can discuss your feelings openly, you're ready to proceed to Step 2.

The purpose of Step 2 is to give your subordinate an opportunity for self-appraisal. Ask him to take a blank pad of paper; label the first sheet Accomplishments; the second sheet Strengths; the third sheet Uncertainties and Misunderstandings; the fourth sheet Obstacles; and the fifth sheet Improvements.

On Sheet 1, Accomplishments, ask him to list all the things he has done in the past year that he is proud of. In what ways did he exceed his own expectations or those of others? Did he solve any unusually difficult problems? Did he do anything he felt others would have difficulty doing? By whose standards

FIGURE 5
The helping appraisal process.

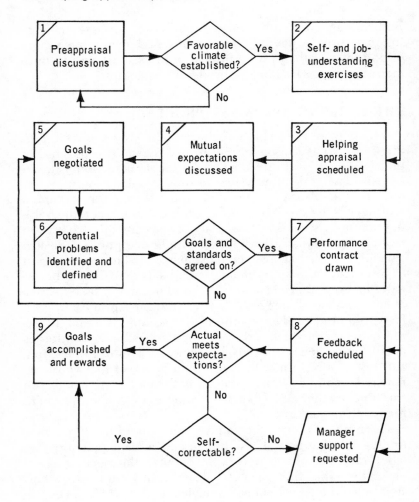

does he feel he excelled? Advise him not to be modest, bragging but not exaggerating.

On the sheet labeled Strengths, ask him to list areas in which he feels he possesses major knowledge, has outstanding skills, or believes he is highly experienced. Explain that it's important that he link these strengths with his accomplishments, showing how they helped him to achieve them. Also, ask him to consider how he can build on these same strengths in the future.

On Sheet 3, Uncertainties and Misunderstandings, ask him to give possible explanations for aspects of his performance that he believes were less than outstanding. He should pay particular attention to factors he felt were beyond his control. Did he receive confusing or vague instructions? Did anybody interfere with his performance? Was there a significant change in external factors that created problems for him? Did somebody he was depending on disappoint him? In what ways did things go wrong that he did not anticipate beforehand? Were there any areas in which he was uncertain about what was expected of him? Did he misunderstand the expectations of others? Was he uncertain about his own ability to accomplish what was expected of him?

Explain that the self-appraisal information is for his own use during the helping appraisal. If he chooses to, he can keep it private; he doesn't have to share it with you. Emphasize that this exercise will enable him to get the most out of the helping appraisal.

On the sheet labeled Obstacles, ask him to list anything or anybody who might interfere with his performance in the future. In what ways might they interfere? Is it likely without any special action on his part that these obstacles will be removed? What kind of help might he need to clear these obstacles?

Finally on the last sheet labeled Improvements, ask him to list ways in which he feels he might improve his methods, relationships, knowledge, skills, behavior, attitudes, and so forth. If he can make these improvements, will they have a positive effect on his performance? Can he make them by himself, or will he need assistance? If so, what kind of assistance? What major changes in the way he performs his job or is allowed to perform his job does he believe will benefit both him and the company?

After preparing these lists, ask him to put them aside for a minimum of one month at which time you review them again. At that time, he'll have an opportunity to make additions to or deletions from the list. If he feels satisfied that the lists are complete and that they accurately reflect his feelings, he should contact you to schedule a helping appraisal. He should do this in writing and should include an agenda of special topics he would like to discuss. Your reply should include the schedule for a specific date and time and a complete agenda, as well as the items he requested plus anything else you want to discuss.

In Step 4, start the helping appraisal with a review of your subordinate's performance plans. What does he want to do during the next year? What does he expect to accomplish? How do his expectations compare with yours? During this discussion, he will probably want to refer to his self-appraisal information and may decide to share it with you.

This discussion of expectations leads to Step 5, the negotiation of goals. What specifically do you both agree are reasonable performance goals and personal goals for the new year? Be certain that these are specific and measurable and that they represent meaningful contributions, fully utilize your subordinate's talents, and are reasonable.

Before finalizing goals and the standards, proceed to Step 6: the identification and definition of potential problems that might interfere with the performance of these goals. Hopefully, your subordinate already prepared a listing of potential problems during the self-appraisal exercise. If he has done that job thoroughly, all you have to do is help him to challenge them, define them fully, and consider their impact on his future performance. Also, because some of the problems may involve you directly, your awareness of them is a good first step toward their solution.

If you both agree on performance goals and standards, you're ready to proceed to Step 7: drawing up a performance contract. If not, you have to renegotiate goals and standards until you are mutually satisfied.

Step 7 is the most critical step in the helping appraisal process. As you can see from the sample performance contract in Figure 6, it contains a description of what your subordinate and you agree to do, as well as specific conditions you both agree to abide by. Let's listen to an abbreviated dialog between the subordinate and manager who prepared the performance contract in Figure 6:

FIGURE 6
The performance contract.

Date _____ *October 1, 1977* _____

Between _____ *T.L., Product manager* _____ and _____ *R.D., Group product manager* _____

Subordinate agrees to:

1. Key area _____ *Developing promotional programs* _____

Expected results	Standards
Performance objectives achieved:	*direct measurement;*
10% increase in product net sales and profits. Increase in: awareness and recall, 15%; market share, 2%; distribution, 10%	*quarterly awareness and recall studies; monthly audit data*

.
.

.

5. Key area _____ *Recommending sales forecasts* _____

Expected results	Standards
Performance objectives achieved:	*±5% variation between*
Product sales forecasts avoided under/overproduction and maintained normal inventories. Aided in setting realistic sales goals for salespeople.	*actual and forecast sales; 12-week inventory of finished goods and 8-week inventory of components and raw materials; number of field complaints less than 2% of sales force.*

Manager agrees to:

1. *Approve increase in product advertising budget.*
.

.

4. *Arrange for special sales forecasting training of product manager.*
5. *Authorization of purchase of computer time-sharing sales forecasting services.*

Both parties agree to following conditions:

1. *No changes in the terms of this contract without consent of both parties in writing.*
2. *Renegotiate terms of contract in the event of significant unforeseen circumstances.*
.

.

5. *Review performance progress quarterly on January 1st, April 1st, July 1st, October 1st, 1978.*

Signed _____ *T.L.* _____

Signed _____ *R.D.* _____

Manager: Now that we have agreed on your goals and have discussed potential problems and how we'll deal with them, we are ready to draw up a performance contract.

Subordinate: A performance contract?

Manager: It's just a written summary of our agreements. It defines carefully what we both agree to do so that at a future date when we sit down to discuss your performance, there's no question about what we both had planned.

Subordinate: Does the contract have to be in any special form, or use legal language?

Manager: No. We can start with a blank piece of paper and describe in our own words what you agree to, what I agree to, and any special conditions we arrange jointly. Let's start with the list of things you said you wanted to accomplish. We'll record them one at a time, listing first the general or key area in which you have formulated an objective, the outcome or expected results if you are successful, and the standards we'll use for measuring results.

Subordinate: Well, at the top of my list is a general objective of developing promotional programs. If my performance objectives are achieved in this key area, the products I manage will have a 10 percent increase in net sales profit. Also, there'll be a 15 percent increase in customer awareness and recall; the product will increase its market share by 2 percent; and 10 percent more wholesalers and retailers will carry the product in inventory.

Manager: How will you measure the achievement of these performance objectives?

Subordinate: Sales and profit can be measured directly from our monthly accounting reports, and market share and distribution can be measured from monthly audit data. To measure awareness and recall, I'll arrange with the market research department to conduct a quarterly awareness and recall study. We'll use the past year's awareness and recall data as baseline information.

The subordinate, in this case a product manager, with the help of his boss, a group product manager, decides to list only five objectives on which they will focus their joint attention. Naturally other responsibilities will not be listed as they will be performed by the product manager. However, the focus of the contract is on areas of improvement. Let's continue the dialog as the product manager lists his last objective.

Subordinate: My fifth objective is in the key area of recommending sales forecasts. If I achieve my performance objective in this area, my product sales forecasts will be accurate enough that I'll avoid any over- and underproduction and will succeed in maintaining normal inventories. Also, my sales forecasts will be accurate enough to allow sales management to set realistic sales goals for our salesmen. The standard for the sales forecasts should be plus or minus 5 percent variation between actual and forecasted sales. We can track them by direct measurement on financial reports. Also, inventories can be measured directly.

Manager: Shouldn't you define what you mean by "normal inventories"?

Subordinate: By normal inventories I mean the usual company policy of a 12-week inventory of finished goods and an 8-week inventory of components and raw material.

Manager: How are you going to measure what the sales department judges to be realistic forecasts?

Subordinate: That's not easy to measure. No matter how carefully I forecast, I know there'll be some field complaints.

Manager: Field complaints? Why not develop a standard for the number of field complaints considered acceptable by sales management? Check with them and ask them to help you to establish a standard. Let's arbitrarily put on the contract less than 2 percent. You can verify it later.

Subordinate: That completes my part of the agreement. Now it's your turn.

Manager: The first thing I agreed to was to approve a 10 percent increase in your product advertising budget. All of your performance objectives are dependent on that increase in advertising. If for any reason that increase is not approved, we'll renegotiate your performance objectives.

The manager lists things he has agreed to in order to support his subordinate. In this case, no special standards are listed because the nature of the manager's agreements are such that the measurement is obvious. Let's continue the dialog at the point in which the manager is listing the things he will do to support his subordinate in the area of sales forecasting.

Manager: As we discussed, I'll arrange for you to attend, within the next few weeks, a 3-day course given by the American Management Associations. You felt uncertain about your skills in the area of forecasting, particularly in using the computer as an aid. The course should help you feel more confident in this area. Finally, I'll authorize the purchase of computer time-sharing so you can take advantage of the special sales forecasting software that is available to strengthen your forecasting.

Subordinate: Does that complete our performance contract?

Manager: No. If you recall, during our discussion our agreements have been based on specific conditions. First, we agreed that there would be no changes in the terms of this contract without the consent of both of us in writing. We spent a lot of time in preparing this contract and therefore should not make changes lightly. However, the contract must be flexible, so let's include a second condition that we will renegotiate the terms of the contract in the event of significant unforeseen circumstances.

Both subordinate and manager contribute to the listing of special conditions. In this case they conclude with a final condition.

Manager: The last condition is that we will review your performance progress quarterly. Let's say January 1st, April 1st, July 1st, and October 1st. This will give us an opportunity to see if we both see eye to eye on the things we've agreed to. At that time, depending on how you're progressing, we may decide to either add or delete items in the contract.

Generally, when you draw up a contract you must make certain that it is mutually rewarding and that your subordinate consents to it voluntarily. If he feels he's been pressured into any of the items he's agreed to, he won't feel committed to live up to his terms—later he'll find a way to break the contract. Moreover, neither of you should agree to any terms you don't feel completely capable of meeting. Because the objective of the contract is improvement, your subordinate may have to stretch somewhat to meet the terms, but he should be reasonably able to do so. Finally, there should be no misrepresentation by either of you. The contract should be drawn up in good faith.

The next step in the appraisal process, Step 8, is scheduling timely feedback. This will help both you and your subordinate to check on his progress. Ideally, the feedback will be received early so that he has sufficient time to correct his actions appropriately. You'll receive the same information simultaneously but will wait a reasonable period of time to allow him to make corrections without your interference. Of course, if it seems likely that he is not going to react to negative feedback, you'll have to bring it to his attention and ask what he's going to do. In this way, you're allowing him to exercise self-control, but are not losing control. For example, after several months the gap between your subordinate's forecast and actual sales results has been widening. As a result, you note from production and inventory reports that there has been overproduction and that inventories have been building up. At the quarterly review, you discuss this problem with your subordinate. He advises you that the first awareness and recall study recorded a high score and that audit data show a depletion in field inventories. This should be reflected shortly in factory sales. Obviously, the new promotions are working, so no special action is necessary at this time.

If all performance objectives are being met, or your subordinate is handling variances effectively, additional help from you, other than what you've already agreed to in the contract, will be obviated. However, if your subordinate is experiencing problems in meeting his objectives, he should feel free to request support. You should be accessible and your services made available as needed. Naturally, you should not assume the burden of your subordinate's problems, but you should be prepared to give guidance when he asks for it, or on occasion, you may feel compelled to intervene. In that case, your intervention should be based on mounting evidence that your subordinate either is not going to live up to the terms of the contract or is incapable of doing so.

The final step in the appraisal process is Step 9, the accomplishment of goals and appropriate rewards. If your subordinate meets all the terms of the contract, he should receive rewards, monetary and nonmonetary, which you have mutually agreed to in advance. In this way, there's no question that he's receiving too much or too little for his efforts.

ADVANTAGES of the HELPING APPRAISAL

In separate interviews with pairs of managers and subordinates who had participated in helping appraisals, I became convinced that it had distinct advantages over conventional appraisals. These are some of their representative comments.

MANAGER COMMENTS

The helping appraisal makes my job easier. I don't have to work to convince my subordinate to improve; he searches for areas in which he can improve and convinces himself to undertake these improvements.

I felt it really strengthened our relationship. For the first time, we leveled with one another and surfaced long-standing misunderstandings. Until I conducted my first helping appraisal, I never realized how resentful some of my subordinates were about past appraisals.

It was a lot easier on both of us. Because we were focusing on objectives and I wasn't in the uncomfortable position of being a judge, we talked freely and we both felt more relaxed than we had in previous appraisals.

I felt for the first time that my subordinate was really motivated to improve his performance. In the past, I felt subordinates were giving me lip service, whereas during helping appraisals, I sensed a genuine feeling of commitment.

During the helping appraisal, when we talked about weaknesses that my subordinate himself had identified, I felt we were engaged in a constructive effort. In the past, when I had identified weaknesses, I felt that doing so, I was being destructive, actually making it harder for my subordinate to improve.

The helping appraisal is rational and systematic. It helped both of us to clarify assignments, expected results, standards, rewards, and a lot of other things we had not spelled out previously. I think we both came away from it with a more realistic understanding of what we expected from each other.

SUBORDINATE COMMENTS

It made me feel good. It wasn't disturbing; it wasn't threatening. I left my boss's office feeling that we understood each other better than we ever had.

This appraisal was held for my benefit. Instead of getting criticized, I got help according to my needs and wants. That's quite a contrast from the kind of appraisals I was used to.

Instead of rehashing the past, we talked about the future. That made a lot of sense to me. I couldn't do anything about the past, but I could certainly do something about the future.

As the appraisal progressed, I found myself more willing to discuss my weaknesses. It was almost as if we were talking about a third person. I didn't feel defensive, because I felt there were no penalties for admitting weaknesses. On the contrary, by doing so, I would get help in overcoming them.

I felt we were equals. My boss and I were working side by side to solve my problems and help me improve my performance. He wasn't telling me what to do, and his opinion didn't have any greater weight than mine.

By the end of the interview, I knew exactly what my boss expected of me. And in the future, I would know how I stand at all times. That's a hell of a lot better than trying to second-guess your boss.

During this appraisal, I really got a fair hearing. It was a two-way conversation instead of the usual monolog. And I felt we were both making reasonable concessions. He was really trying to understand my point of view and address my needs and wants.

TOO GOOD TO BE TRUE?

I don't blame you if you feel skeptical about all these glowing comments. Not all helping appraisals work out so well. In fact, some of them end up as disasters. That's because it requires a considerable amount of skill and practice to conduct an effective helping appraisal. It also requires a 180-degree change in your attitudes about the purpose of appraisals and how they should be conducted, and switching from evaluating to helping is a very difficult transition. Furthermore, some managers just can't establish the rapport and level of trust that are critical to the helping appraisal. These managers feel uncomfortable not being able to retreat behind their shield of authority and really don't want to completely level with their subordinates.

Sometimes managers have difficulty getting approval to use helping appraisals. They function in a work environment that is difficult to change and are thus forced to conduct conventional annual performance appraisals. In these situations, I suspect many companies are flexible enough to allow a manager to experiment with the helping appraisal, particularly in working with nonpromotables. At the very least, they are likely to allow a parallel appraisal system—the helping appraisal to meet the subordinate's needs and the conventional appraisal to fulfill administrative requirements.

Over the years, the nonpromotable has learned to fear and resent the conventional performance appraisal. And why not, since he associates missed promotional opportunities with bad performance appraisals? It's hard to convince him that he'll derive any benefits from it. And it's doubtful that the appraisal will teach him much about his weaknesses or motivate him to try to correct them. He's heard it all before and hasn't done anything about it.

In contrast to conventional appraisals, the helping appraisal offers a significant change. The subordinate is not being forced to change himself or his work habits; rather, he's being offered help, if he decides positively, to change and improve his performance and thereby improve the quality of his work life. That's a good deal—nothing to lose and everything to gain.

CHAPTER SEVEN

Redirecting
Aging Careers

THE DOWNHILL SIDE

Chapter 1 describes the "fixation stage" of nonpromotability as being time-related, usually occurring in one's forties, fifties, and the final preretirement years. By this stage, everyone, including those who try to ignore reality, has become aware that his or her aspirations will not be attained. That realization is accompanied by a sense of frustration and disappointment.

For many people, this is referred to as the "downhill" side of their career. A major symptom is preoccupation with their advancing age. Gray hair can be colored, and diet and exercise can retard the aging process, but both physiologically and psychologically older employees simply cannot deny unwanted bodily changes. And, in many cases, bouts with ill health serve to remind them of their mortality. The phrase, "I don't seem to be able to . . . " is repeated to himself and to others as the aging employee recognizes his progressing limitations.

Both at home and at work, the downhill side of one's career offers a series of setbacks. At home, there's often a weakening of family bonds. A situation like the following one is common:

I have three children—a son who's a senior in high school, another son who's a junior in college, and a married daughter. They are all busy with their own lives. Except for holidays, we're rarely together

as a family unit. We used to spend a lot of time together. And the
children used to listen to what I had to say and seemed to enjoy my
company. Now, they tend to ignore my advice and only occasionally
show any appreciation for me. Even my wife is less attentive and appears to be less interested in me.

At work, disturbing changes are also taking place. Instead of
being the bright "comer," many older workers start thinking
of themselves as "has-beens." They question the time they've
spent with the company and the purpose and importance of
their job. But they recognize that they have less mobility than
in the past, because they are not as attractive in the job market.
Like it or not, there's no place else to go. As one older worker
complained to me during a counseling interview: "I'm no
longer in the prime of my life or the prime of my career. From
now on, the best I can hope for is to try to slow down my personal losses."

Understandably, it's difficult to manage employees who
believe the passing of time threatens to create new discomfort,
disappointments, and defeats. They tend to resist change
because they're fearful of it. This can make them inflexible, as
shown by the following dialog.

> *Manager:* I've decided to change our methods of reporting. I
> don't feel I'm getting the right kind of information fast enough
> to take appropriate action.
>
> *Subordinate:* We've been using the present system for years,
> and I've never heard any complaints in the past.
>
> *Manager:* I know we've been using it for years. And, yes, it was
> useful. But our business has changed and so have our informa-
> tional needs.
>
> *Subordinate:* I don't see any sense in changing a good system
> that has proved workable over time. Besides, I'm used to using
> it.

In addition to fear of change, employees in the fixation stage
of their careers tend to have a high level of anxiety. They're
concerned that they may be losing their competence and
becoming obsolete. They worry that they will no longer be
considered valued employees and that they will lose status
and position, or worse yet, get tossed out into an inhospitable

job market. Because of these feelings, they're less willing to take risks and try to avoid accountability, as shown by this example:

> *Manager:* Jim, I don't understand the way you've been acting lately. You're the senior man in our group and normally I would expect you to express strong opinions in our staff meetings. Instead, you seem to hold back and follow the lead of the group.
>
> *Subordinate:* [Being evasive and defensive] I haven't changed, except perhaps to give the younger men an opportunity to express their own opinions. I feel that if I speak up too early, I'll influence them. Also, I don't want to rush into making any rash opinions until I have sufficient facts.
>
> *Manager:* That certainly wasn't your style in the past. You were always one of the first men to speak up.
>
> *Subordinate:* Frankly [confiding in his boss], in the past I didn't give a damn if I stepped on other people's toes or talked out of turn. Now that I'm getting older, and have less options open to me, I feel I have to be more careful about what I say and do.

Frequently, senior employees feel angry and guilty about life and career goals they no longer believe they can obtain. They're angry because they feel they deserve more for their efforts; guilty because they feel they have shortchanged their families and themselves by not living up to their aspirations. They keep replaying the same record: "Perhaps if I had tried harder, done things differently, or had more luck, I could have gotten more out of my life and my career." These frustrating feelings often lead to confrontations:

> *Manager.* For someone with as many years' experience as you have, I'm not satisfied with your performance lately.
>
> *Subordinate.* I think I give the company more than it deserves, considering how I've been mistreated.
>
> *Manager.* Mistreated?
>
> *Subordinate.* After all the years I've spent with this company, I should be in a higher position and making much more money. I've worked hard in the past and what has it gotten me?

The anger that senior employees feel is often suppressed, as it's dangerous to let it out in open confrontation. Instead, it is usually manifested in the form of general irritability and over-sensitivity, often directed toward younger peers:

Younger Employee. I'm having trouble understanding how to complete this procedure. Can you give me some help?

Senior Employee. I don't have time to do your job and my job too.

Younger Employee. I'm not asking you to do my job. I just would like some advice. You have much more experience than I, and you might be able to save me a great deal of time with hardly any effort on your part.

Senior Employee. Why don't you try learning the way I did — by trial and error. You young people are always looking for the easy way out.

One characteristic of senior employees that makes them very difficult to manage is defensiveness. They don't like to admit errors or magnify their importance. Instead, they attempt to rationalize mistakes or blame others for them:

Manager. Your inventory levels are too high.

Subordinate. It's not my fault [rationalizing]. I got faulty information from the marketing research department [projecting his own blame to someone else].

Manager. But aren't you responsible for watching the actual weekly flow of units in and out of inventory? Market research data are just reported to help you compare actual factory sales with consumer movement in the market.

Subordinate [Rationalizing and denying the truth]. My work load has been extraordinarily heavy, and I've been receiving EDP reports late. I do the best I can under the circumstances.

Finally, another reaction to the changes that accompany an aging career is the "downhill blues." Accumulating disappointments, defeats, and rejections tend to sap the energy of many senior employees. They feel sorry for themselves and regret their lost opportunities. If severe enough, their depression can completely immobilize them and threaten their health. One concerned manager expressed his observations on this attitude to the personnel manager:

Manager. I don't know what to do about Charlie. He only goes through the motions of doing his job. He's frequently late and absent. Most of the time, he looks like something's bothering him, but I can't get him to open up and talk to me. Also, he always looks tired, like he hasn't been sleeping. And, he's become careless about his personal grooming.

Personnel Manager. I'll talk to him, and if I feel I can't help him —perhaps we ought to refer him to a physician. It sounds like he's suffering from depression. Ever since we had one of our men commit suicide, I don't like to take any chances with someone who seems to be suffering from prolonged emotional problems.

PLAN for REDIRECTION

Everything seems to be working against the individual stuck in the fixation stage of his career. You are probably becoming as disenchanted with his performance as he is with his job and career. If he continues in the same direction, the situation will probably worsen. That's why, as a manager, it's important for you to develop plans to redirect his career. Figure 7 summarizes the elements of a comprehensive redirec-

FIGURE 7
Plan for redirecting the aging career.

OLD DIRECTION	REDIRECTION
Reflecting on "past glories"	Focus on future
"Waiting out time"	Active quality improvement
"Doing same old thing"	Career changes
Declining performance	Frequent helping appraisals
Primacy of work	Gradual detachment from work
Insecurity	Build self-confidence
Competitiveness	Cooperation
Obsolescence	Training and development
Limitations of aspirations	Alternative career pathing
Isolation	Involvement

tion plan. The following series of cases illustrates how this plan can be put into effect.

1. Ted is the old pro. For many years, he was a leading salesman. However, at age fifty, he's lost some of his energy and drive. And, although he still performs adequately, he is no longer classified in the top third of the sales force. He's become content to talk about the "good old days" and reflect on his "past glories."

To redirect Ted, his manager must get him to focus on the future. He has to appeal to his sense of pride, by showing him how his knowledge, skills, and experience can help him regain his past performance. He works with him to establish short work goals that will allow him to experience success frequently and thus reinforce his renewed efforts.

2. Bill is a purchasing agent for a large company with a reputation for refusing to fire anyone who's been with them for more than ten years. As a 20-year veteran, Bill believes it's unnecessary to extend himself. All he has to do is keep out of trouble and "wait out his time."

Fortunately for him and the company, his manager has different ideas. He intends to get him to change direction by initiating a program of active quality improvement. He refuses to treat Bill as an old-timer past his days of peak performance. Instead, he'll maintain high standards and expectations, forcing him to keep stretching for improvement.

3. Ann is a budget analyst who, for the last ten years, has been doing virtually "the same old things." Boredom seems too mild a term to describe her feelings about her job.

Her manager's plans for her redirection involve a series of lateral career changes. He intends to move her from job to job within the department at least every two years until she retires. He's willing to invest in the frequent retraining, because he recognizes the destructiveness of staying too long in the same job. If at any time it becomes impractical to make a lateral career change, he'll try to restructure the job she's in so that she gets an opportunity for job variety.

4. Edna's performance has been declining steadily over the last five years. She's a programmer in the EDP Department and a highly skilled specialist. Even though she's performing

at a much lower capacity than she did in the past, she still is a very valuable employee.

Her manager plans to upgrade her performance by scheduling frequent helping appraisals, probably at quarterly intervals. Together, they will set future goals and agree on a matching reward system that will encourage her to perform as she has in the past.

5. For Mildred, work is her life. She's unmarried and has worked in the same hospital laboratory for 30 years. Her circle of friends consists entirely of fellow workers. Mildred's job gives her a feeling of status, self-acceptance, self-worth, in addition to being a source of prestige and recognition. It's also a way to pass time. Because of this, she frequently works overtime because she "has nothing else to do." Now that she is approaching retirement, she has become increasingly concerned about the future and has asked her boss several times about the possibility of working past the compulsory retirement age.

Her manager recognizes the need to redirect Mildred's dependence on work. She has planned a series of counseling sessions during which time she will attempt to gradually detach Mildred from her work interests. Together, they'll explore areas in which her outside interests can be expanded, and from which she can derive some of the important needs provided for by her current job. She feels it's her obligation as a manager to help Mildred make this transition.

6. Henry is insecure because he is, as he sarcastically acknowledges, "the oldest living product manager." He's 59 years old and a manager of major brands for a large toiletries company. All of the other product managers he works with are in their early to mid-thirties. Although he does his job well and is well regarded by his boss, he comes to work each day waiting for "the ax to fall." This insecurity has made him reluctant to take risks and fixed in his work habits.

His manager plans to redirect him by building his sense of importance, using him as a sounding board, encouraging the other product managers to seek his advice, using him to train and develop the other product managers, and demonstrating in every way he can that he values his services and respects him.

7. Although Stan knows he's no longer in consideration for promotion, he still competes fiercely with the other men in his department. He's determined to prove that age has not slowed him down, and that he's "as good as he ever was." Unfortunately, in so doing, he has alienated his colleagues and is frequently the center of controversy. He is particularly resentful of the younger men and goes out of his way to make them look bad.

His manager wants to turn Stan into an asset instead of a liability. He feels he can do this by involving him in enforced group activities in which he can derive recognition only from group results. Also, he has entrusted him directly with responsibility for the results of several of the younger men. His manager deliberately withholds recognition for his individual performance, but is quick to praise and reward him when he behaves in a helping role, providing guidance to others and sharing his knowledge and experience with them.

8. Jim is an engineer working for a high technology company. He started becoming obsolete years ago, but was unwilling to admit what was happening to him. Instead, he has become a master of covering up his deficiencies and depending on the younger engineers to help him to "hang on to his job." However, he's finding it increasingly difficult to do so.

His manager recognizes what's been happening to him. To help redirect his course, he has planned a complete "retreading" program. It involves the comprehensive assessment of his present knowledge and skills, as well as a systematic program to upgrade them. He'll be encouraged to attend workshops and return to school in an evening program, and will receive special on-the-job training. In addition, his manager will consider redesigning his job so that he can spend more time working in areas in which he is competent or can be retrained with relative ease.

9. Joan has been a hard-driving, ambitious performer throughout her career. Until about five years ago, she was rewarded for her efforts with regular advancements. Now she feels frustrated because she has been passed over for promotion, and realizes that she has probably reached the highest level of her capabilities. Nevertheless, she finds it difficult to change a lifelong record of striving for advancement.

Knowing how important it is for Joan to feel a sense of challenge and career momentum, her manager is planning a series of alternative career paths for her. These are lateral moves, but they will provide her with an opportunity for new learning, challenge, variety, and a sense of accomplishment and importance.

10. Gloria feel neglected by her manager. Although she doesn't receive any less attention than the other people in her department, she feels she has been put on the shelf and forgotten. She's resentful and dreads the years ahead until her retirement.

In his redirection planning, her manager recognizes her strong need for companionship and reassurance. He plans to give her special attention, meeting with her informally on a frequent basis. Also, he plans to involve her in several intradepartmental and interdepartmental committees to give her a strong feeling of involvement.

As these cases illustrate, a concerned manager can help redirect destructive behavior patterns of senior employees by diagnosing their individual needs and then using a variety of methods to try to fulfill them. In addition, he tries to share their concerns with them, by engaging in frequent counseling sessions and demonstrating that he values them by giving them attention and understanding. This special handling does not include lower performance expectations. If anything, he does them a disservice by not expecting them to perform as well as younger people. He encourages them to grow and provides opportunity for learning and developing. He helps them recapture some of the waning energy and interest they had early in their careers. And he accepts an obligation for helping them make the difficult transition from work to retirement.

HELPING the OLDER EMPLOYEE
to CAPITALIZE on HIS AGE

Much of the discussion in this chapter and in management literature in general centers on the liabilities associated with age. However, there are substantial positive aspects of aging that can serve as a foundation for coping with the negative aspects. This is particularly true for older employees who have not only become chronologically mature, but who are psychologically mature.

The older employee has had more years and experiences in which to get to know himself and establish his values and priorities. This self-awareness is important in accepting himself, others, and the work situation. He has learned to expect surprises in life and to adapt to them. Younger employees often lack both the same tolerance for undesirable surprises and the capacity for adaptation.

One advantage of spending years within the same organization is that you "learn the ropes." The employee with longevity should know how to get things done within your specific work environment. He knows who's influential in decision making. He knows how to make efficient use of intracompany resources. He knows how to work within and around policies and procedures. And he's in a better position to recognize changes in the environment because he has a longer historical frame of reference.

One of the biggest assets he should have is the good will he has banked over the years. He has worked hard to build strong relationships with many people at all levels of the organization. When he needs allies either for personal support or for programs he advocates, he should have a full reservoir of friends.

Over the years, he should have compiled a record of accomplishments. He knows what he does well because he has demonstrated his strengths. The accumulated knowledge and skills can serve him well as a foundation for new learning. As long as he is committed to personal growth, he has skills that are transferable to new assignments and challenges.

As an elder statesman, he should command respect. He represents organizational continuity. He knows how the organization came to its current status, as well as what worked and what didn't work. He should possess wisdom that comes with having had a variety of different experiences and exposure to a multiplicity of problems and decisions. He's far less easy to disrupt than are employees who are newer on the scene. The combination of having "been there before" and psychological maturity can be an extraordinary asset during a crisis situation.

One of his strongest assets stems from what could be regarded as a liability—his lack of upward mobility. Because he is no longer competing for advancement, the pressure is off him to "look good." He doesn't have to impress anybody to gain competitive advantage over somebody else. Instead, he can concentrate on getting the job done and on truly helping others to advance. In contrast to the egocentricity of the ambitious younger employee, he can afford to be more gracious, concerned, caring, and understanding of others.

The manager who has responsibility for the supervision of senior employees should consider both the positive and negative aspects of aging and its effect in the work situation. To help redirect the future employment of these employees, he should focus on helping them to look ahead instead of backward. Most importantly, he should take advantage of their age, rather than believe that they are handicapped by it.

CHAPTER EIGHT

Untangling Destructive Mismatches

The nonpromotable can do much to help himself gain work satisfaction. But sometimes he becomes so entangled in destructive mismatches that it takes heroic action to extricate him. He may be mismatched with his current job, you, and/or his work situation. As his manager, you can intervene in meaningful ways, but you can't help someone who may not want to or be able to respond to advice and guidance.

ENTANGLING ALLIANCES

Job Mismatches

> Maybe I shouldn't have promoted him. He was a great salesman, but he's been a poor performer since he accepted a higher-level job.

The lament of this manager, who confided in me that his selection error may have contributed to a mismatch, was that he had made a mistake. All too often, when confronted with a failing subordinate, managers react by applying increased pressure in an effort to force him to "shape up," rather than admit they picked the wrong man for the job. But the effect of the added pressure runs counter to its intended purpose — the subordinate's performance deteriorates at a faster rate.

When a subordinate doesn't respond to repeated coaching, yet seems to be trying hard to follow your directions, ask yourself: What are the essential specifications for his job? Does he have the basic qualifications to satisfy these specifications? Can I help him fill gaps in his skills and experience? Are his deficiencies remediable?

Perhaps your subordinate was qualified initially for his job, but the job has outgrown him. This happens frequently to people in highly technical jobs who fail to keep up to date with rapidly changing technology. Furthermore, the demands of the job may have increased substantially because of special conditions, such as extraordinary company growth, competitive activities, new responsibilities resulting from reorganization, and so forth.

To determine if a subordinate's job has outgrown him, ask yourself: In what ways have the specifications of his job changed since he was first hired? What has he done to satisfy the new requirements of the job? What have I done to prepare him for increased responsibilities?

Another common employee–job mismatch develops when your subordinate becomes "overripe." He has mastered his job and feels it's not challenging him any more. He has outgrown his job.

In earlier chapters, I described ways in which to help a non-promotable who has outgrown his job. Obviously, these methods won't work with every subordinate. After you have given him a reasonable trial, ask yourself: In what ways, if any, have I helped him? Does he appear to be searching for ways to make his job more satisfying? Is he trying to discard undesirable attitudes and behavior? Is his performance improving?

Managerial Mismatches

A subordinate may resist your efforts to help him if *you* are the reason for his job dissatisfaction. Perhaps it's an oil-and-water situation — you and he just don't mix. He has personality traits that are immiscible with yours, which results in frequent clashes. For example, you may be independent and forceful, whereas he's dependent and timid. You want him to behave as you do, and he can't.

In contrast, a subordinate whose personality is too similar to yours may be a mismatch. For example, if your subordinate is as independent and forceful as you, he may resent taking orders and try to circumvent them.

Whether diametrically opposed or similar, strong personality traits can lead to strong differences in opinion. Eventually your work relationship can deteriorate to the point at which you become adversaries who compete with each other rather than collaborate.

Also contributing to an adversary relationship are such factors as differing perceptions, values, needs, and wants. Conflicts may develop because you and your subordinate don't see things in the same way. Perhaps he has strong social values, and has a need to help others and be accepted by them. Yet, as a supervisor who reports to you, he is expected to achieve company objectives. To satisfy your expectations, he may have to act in a way that his subordinates won't like. In so doing he will have to compromise his own values as well as make demands he perceives as unwarranted. Obviously, he may decide not to try to satisfy your expectations.

Another source of friction between you and your subordinate is related to your style of management. You and he may disagree on the amount of autonomy he should have. Once again, if no match exists for your respective feelings and opinions, misunderstandings and conflict will develop. He may expect, for example, that his job seniority warrants light direction and control and democratic leadership. (You're accustomed to giving heavy direction and control and limited freedom of action.) On the other hand, he may prefer to take orders, follow directions, and be watched over by an autocratic manager. (You want to be able to delegate responsibility, spend minimum direct supervisory time with him, and manage democratically.)

Sometimes bad past experiences sour a healthy subordinate–manager match. Perhaps he has lost respect for you; he believes you misdirect him and inhibit his effectiveness. He's convinced you don't know how to manage. He feels you're insensitive, uninterested, inconsistent, unfair, and nonsupportive. This view was expressed to me in a counseling interview in which a disenchanted subordinate complained about his manager:

Four years ago when he took charge of the department, I was delighted. He had an excellent reputation and I was looking forward to working with him. What everyone neglected to tell me about him is that he earned his reputation by being ruthless. Nothing mattered to him except exceeding objectives. On many occasions, he told me that he expected my complete loyalty and full commitment. But it wasn't a reciprocal arrangement.

At first, I tried to give him a 100 percent effort. But in return, he kept loading me with new assignments and pressuring me for greater productivity—and I got the same salary increases as other men in the department who were coasting along. I didn't get any special recognition for breaking my back for him. Naturally, after a year of this kind of one-sided relationship, I lost my respect for him and my enthusiasm for my job.

Situational Mismatches

Even the right person in the right job working under a competent manager can be confronted by a work climate that's wrong for him. As Figure 8 shows, specific characteristics of a work climate can be troublesome to vulnerable people.

FIGURE 8
Sources of situational mismatches.

CHARACTERISTICS OF WORK CLIMATE	VULNERABLE PEOPLE
Cliques	Overly sensitive and gregarious
Rivalries	Psychologically injured; immature
Changeability	Insecure; inflexible
Intolerance	Mentally and/or physically ill; imprudent
Conformity	Creative and independent; individualistic

Cliques. In a work climate characterized by cliques, a subordinate who is overly sensitive and gregarious is vulnerable.

He's friendly and outgoing and wants to belong, but the cliques are tightly organized groups that don't welcome outsiders. Eventually, his feelings of isolation and rejection will hurt his performance.

Rivalries. A work climate in which rivalries flourish is unhealthy for psychologically injured and immature subordinates. The psychologically injured bear scars of past rivalries. They've fought battles and lost, and are therefore fearful of future encounters. They restrict their activities to safe areas and won't openly express an opinion that might be interpreted as taking sides in a rivalry. The immature subordinates are too impulsive and emotional to avoid rivalries. They're usually in the middle of them, battling continually. But whether they try to circumvent rivalries or are naturally attracted to them, individuals caught in these situations are seriously disrupted by them.

Changeability. A changeable work climate can become unbearable for insecure and inflexible subordinates. Many subordinates, particularly those who are nonpromotable, function best with the status quo. They resist the changes a business has to make to adjust to its external environment. They're unhappy when old friends leave and are replaced by strangers. They worry about relatively minor changes in company policy and procedure, and they panic about major ones. Any change is viewed with alarm.

In a volatile environment, these insecure and inflexible people feel threatened continually. Rapid turnover and frequent reorganization keep them wary and off balance.

Unfortunately, they remain the only constant in an ever-changing work situation. As time passes they become even more sensitized to change in an unsuccessful struggle to control it.

Intolerance. Another work climate that can be unhealthy for individuals with specific vulnerabilities is one characterized by intolerance for people with "weaknesses." This environment is unaccepting of the social casualties of life—those who have acquired alcoholic or drug problems, nervous disorders, or even chronic physical ailments. No attempt is made to understand these people, to support them, or to accommodate temporarily while they're rehabilitating.

The same intolerance is directed at people judged to have acted in an imprudent manner. The standards of impropriety are not well defined and may range from getting drunk at an office function to committing an unethical or illegal act. Regardless of the degree of severity, the work climate can become extremely inhospitable. Past records are ignored and violators are reminded continually about their transgressions.

Conformist pressures. A final situational mismatch results when nonconformists are confronted by a work climate characterized by conformity. They may fight openly for their individuality or make a pretense of being cooperative while resisting conformity covertly.

Subordinates who are creative, independent, and individualistic are highly valued by some companies, but in other companies they're unwelcome. Their refusal to follow the "rules" can create problems for them as well as for you. You become the man in the middle, defending company rules that you may or may not endorse. You are forced to repress their individuality, and they feel stymied.

When their resistance isn't open, they can do considerable damage before you realize that they're "fighting the system." They influence others under your supervision, which not only escalates their personal problems but also succeeds in making others discontented.

PROBABLE OUTCOME of MISMATCHES

Time frames may differ, but the course and outcome of a mismatch are predictable. The first indication of a mismatch is your feeling that your subordinate is discontented. He may verbalize these feelings or manifest them by the way in which he performs his job. Eventually, you begin to feel displeased with what you consider a less than full effort and perceive as a negative attitude.

Here's how a mismatched subordinate may behave, as told by his disheartened manager:

He acted as it he couldn't shift out of second gear. Nothing seemed to excite him and he performed in a perfunctory way. He didn't confide in me and tell me what was bothering him, but he was sending nonverbal messages all the time — raised eyebrows and grimaces. He would also drop wisecracks and ask pseudo-questions, challenging the validity or relevance of assignments.

Ultimately, your gut reaction that something is wrong is confirmed by actual crises. For one thing, a mismatched subordinate may precipitate a crisis by becoming increasingly arrogant and hostile toward you and others. He becomes a troublemaker. But more often, a subordinate's performance will simply deteriorate to the point of missed deadlines, inaccuracies, insufficient productivity. At this point, you decide either to take action or to let his performance slide until your superior demands that you intervene.

You know that your other subordinates, peers, and superiors are watching how you'll handle the crisis. If you wait too long to take action the situation becomes more serious, urgent, and far-reaching. And your delay in acting is interpreted by onlookers as procrastination and indecisiveness. In contrast, if you react too quickly or overreact, you're viewed as precipitate and lacking in self-control.

Thus, crises can lead to inappropriate reactive behavior, which in turn escalates the crises in a spiraling effect. Unless you succeed in stopping its spread and acceleration, the final outcome will be the termination of the mismatched subordinate and any others he may have involved in his problem.

THE COSTS of TERMINATION

Termination of a subordinate may sometimes appear a simple solution, but it can be costly and is rarely uncomplicated. The actual monetary loss includes termination benefits, which can be quite high for long-term employees, in addition to the cost of recruiting and training replacements. For instance, an employee who earns $25,000 a year with 15 years' time with the same company might get over $12,000 in termination benefits. And the cost of recruiting and training a replacement could easily exceed that amount.

Less readily quantifiable, but nevertheless of significant value, are the nonmonetary costs—the effects of termination on others closely related to the person fired, as well as on the manager forced to fire a long-term employee. Such costs are rarely short term.

Even if your decision to terminate a mismatched subordinate is completely justified, and you handle it fairly, friends of the ousted person will probably be critical and resentful of you. You have hurt someone they liked and worked closely with for years. Although they may recognize some of his weaknesses, they usually have tunnel vision, which prevents them from seeing his major failings. Because his friends are emotionally involved with him, they expect you to give him "one more chance."

Furthermore, others less closely related to the ousted person may identify with him. They are usually made aware, either directly or by the grapevine, of the imagined and real hardships that face him and the members of his family. At the traditional leaving-the-company luncheon, they see, feel, and share some of the unhappiness and bitterness he displays. They feel threatened by his termination and tend to reexamine their own relationships with you. This makes them feel less secure and less trustful of you.

You, too, are probably affected by his dismissal. You've known the subordinate and his family for a long time. You were probably friendly with him and liked him personally. You feel guilty that you're hurting him. And you may have some second thoughts about the action you have taken. Perhaps you feel you mishandled him. You may ask yourself, "Did I do all I could to save him? Did I judge him by objective standards, or did I allow my own emotions to influence my decision? Should I have 'carried him' for a longer time?"

Aside from your concern for your subordinate and your own self-doubts and guilt about firing him, you may feel that you "look bad." You worry that your superiors believe you acted too quickly and too strongly. Or you feel that in the eyes of your subordinates, peers, and superiors, you got rid of your subordinate because you weren't strong enough to control him.

Finally, you may sense a feeling of unrest precipitated by the termination. The post-termination atmosphere has been described to me by a number of managers. Typically, their comments sound like this:

I can't understand it. Almost anybody in my shoes would have fired him, yet everybody acts as if I've done something wrong.

People are careful about what they say to me. They appear to be much more subdued and less casual in the way they act toward me.

I can't be specific about the general change in the work atmosphere, but I know it's different. And I don't like the difference.

ALTERNATIVES to TERMINATION

Because termination clearly involves high costs, there are other alternatives you should consider. To help you consider major alternatives, try using Worksheet 6 as an aid.

WORKSHEET 6
Alternatives to termination.

Rate each as positive (+) or negative (−)	Probability of success	Time and resources required	Endorsement by superior	Temporary/permanent results	Reflection on managerial capabilities
Rehabilitate the subordinate					
Change how you feel about him					
Restructure his job					
Restructure the situation					
Demote him					
Transfer him					

Rehabilitation

In previous chapters, I discussed how you can counsel, develop, revitalize, and appraise subordinates. Assuming that you're willing to give these methods a fair trial, maintain a log in which to note signs of responsiveness and positive attitudinal and behavioral changes. After a minimum of six months, estimate the probability of rehabilitating him successfully — very high, high, average, low, or very low. Consider the time and resources — very heavy, heavy, moderate, light, or very light investment — you think will be necessary to bring about desired changes. Are the time and resources available? Can you afford them? What do you think your own superior feels about your management of the failing subordinate? Will he highly endorse, endorse, not endorse, oppose, or strongly oppose your actions? Will you succeed in rehabilitating your subordinate and antagonizing a superior who believes your time could have been spent more productively elsewhere?

Are the subordinate's changes temporary or permanent — definitely permanent, probably permanent, possibly more than temporary, probably temporary, or definitely temporary? Often a subordinate will respond favorably to your extra attention and display of interest. But that response may be short-lived. Periodic reinforcement can sometimes cause temporary changes to become more permanent.

In trying to change a subordinate, are you acting like a professional manager? Will others think you are managing your subordinate very capably, capably, moderately capably, incapably, or very incapably? Are you being fair, flexible, and realistic? Are you overly concerned with the subordinate's interests and your own self-interests, rather than the best interests of the company?

Change of Attitude

Using the same yardsticks and rating scales, consider the probabilty of success if you change your own feelings, the time investment, your superior's view of your actions, the permanency of the changes, and whether the changes reflect favorably on your capabilities as a manager. Of particular significance is your motivation for changing your feelings. If you do so to avoid the unpleasantness of having to confront a subordinate and terminate him, your actions will be viewed unfavorably. However, if your changed feelings demonstrate mastery of your own undesirable attitudes, you enhance your image.

Job/Situation Restructuring

Once again, apply the same yardsticks and ratings. And remember that not only your actions but your motives will influence onlookers' opinions of how well you're satisfying your responsibilities as a manager.

In restructuring jobs and work situations, balance is a key concept. You should try to achieve balance between acceptable and unacceptable levels of experimentation and innovativeness, and between desirable stability and undesirable dynamism.

Demotion and Transfer

The probability of successfully demoting or transferring someone you feel has been unmanageable is generally not high. Also, the likelihood that your superior and others will respect you for unloading your headache, is not very great.

But, if you can salvage someone who has served the company well in the past, and who you feel, in the proper assignment, can resume a productive career, you should accept the risk. If you succeed, you'll rightfully earn the respect and gratitude of the subordinate and interested onlookers.

Terminating someone who can be salvaged is a waste of valuable manpower. Too often, it's a desperate act of an incapable manager.

WHEN to SALVAGE FAILING SUBORDINATES

The questionnaire in Worksheet 7 was designed to help you decide when to try salvaging a failing subordinate. I recommend that you ask someone whose judgment you respect to assist you in completing Parts I and II. Ideally, select a colleague who doesn't have any strong predispositions and who's likely to be objective and independent.

WORKSHEET 7
When to salvage the failing subordinate.

	Yes	No	Don't Know
Date _____			

Determining potential value of _____ *to company:*

1. Has employee performed well prior to past year? ___ ___ ___
2. Does employee have any outstanding strengths that can be useful to company? ___ ___ ___
3. Is employee liked and respected by his peers? ___ ___ ___
4. Has he demonstrated ability to learn from experience and self-develop? ___ ___ ___
5. Does employee have specific experience? ___ ___ ___

Determining difficulties in salvaging employee:

1. Does employee have realistic aspirations? ___ ___ ___
2. Is employee introspective and self-aware, recognizing his own weaknesses? ___ ___ ___
3. Is employee pragmatic and functional? ___ ___ ___
4. Was he content with work situation prior to current difficulties? ___ ___ ___
5. Is employee willing to accept help? ___ ___ ___

Progress reporting:

Initial Counseling

1. Has employee participated actively in mutual problem-solving? ___ ___ ___
2. Has he accepted full responsibility for achieving mutually acceptable goals? ___ ___ ___

30 Days Later

1. Has employee taken first steps toward goals? ___ ___ ___
2. Is he accepting and responding to coaching? ___ ___ ___
3. Is employee beginning to discard undesirable attitudes and behaviors? ___ ___ ___

90 Days Later

1. Is employee enthusiastic and optimistic about achieving goals? ___ ___ ___
2. Has he regressed in any way, repeating past undesirable attitudes and behavior? ___ ___ ___
3. Are the odds better now than 90 days ago that employee's performance will improve substantially? ___ ___ ___

Potential Value to the Company

Because salvaging a failing employee requires an investment in time and probably other resources, you should be certain that you have selected a candidate who has good potential
value to the company. Certainly, you shouldn't try to salvage
anyone who has never been a good performer or who hasn't
performed well for a prolonged period of time. It's probably
too late to rehabilitate him as his behavior patterns have
become relatively fixed.

The candidate should have important strengths that you feel
can, if employed properly, be of value to the company. Naturally, he'll have weaknesses, perhaps uncorrectable ones, but
his strengths should outweigh them.

He should be someone who is liked and respected by his
peers. If you select a candidate who's disliked and not respected, his peers will be critical of you and will not cooperate
with you.

Because your ultimate goal is improved subordinate performance, you should consider candidates who have demonstrated ability to learn from experience and develop themselves. Your role will be to facilitate his learning and
development by guiding and supporting him, and removing
obstacles. But you can't help someone who repeats past mistakes after you've made him aware of them and who is unable
to assume a primary responsibility for helping himself.

Finally, the candidate should be someone who has acquired
special experience which you believe is valuable. If the candidate is someone you can replace readily without concern
about losing the benefits of his experience and know-how,
he's probably not worth salvaging.

Difficulties

Even if a candidate is potentially valuable to the company,
if you believe there's a strong possibility that you won't
succeed in salvaging him, don't waste your time and company
resources. Also, consider risks versus gains. You may want to
accept a greater risk for an extraordinary person. But, even
then, can you afford to bet on long shots?

A primary consideration is the level of aspirations of the employee. If you're dealing with a nonpromotable who's unreal-

istic about his career aspirations, his dissatisfaction with lack of advancement will probably affect his future performance. But, a nonpromotable with realistic aspirations is likely to set achievable goals that can give him satisfaction as well as increase his value to the company.

A lack of realism is often an indication of self-deception. It's difficult to help someone who's unwilling or unable to take a close look at himself and increase his self-awareness. He can't correct weaknesses he doesn't recognize or acknowledge.

Most employees who can be helped readily are pragmatic and functional. Whereas they may be emotionally sidetracked, they understand the necessity of "doing what they have to" in order to function successfully in a specific work environment. You may have to redirect them and help them abandon self-defeating beliefs, behavior, and feelings, but they're adaptable and are likely to follow your lead.

In contrast to these pragmatists, are dysfunctional employees who have been long-term malcontents. A man who has never enjoyed his job, the work climate, and the company is unlikely to respond to anything you do to help him.

Finally, you can't help someone who doesn't want your help and resists it. Perhaps he's overly independent. On the other hand, he may have convinced himself he doesn't deserve help or is beyond helping. In fact, he may even, because of psychological or personal problems, want to fail. He can't be salvaged without a genuine willingness to accept help.

Progress Reporting

Once you've decided that a subordinate is worth salvaging and is likely to be helped, plan a program of changes as needed to untangle mismatches. Launch it during an initial counseling interview. The essential conditions that you must establish are active subordinate participation in mutual problem solving in conjunction with his acceptance of full responsibility for achieving mutually agreed on goals. Start with three or four readily obtainable, but nevertheless significant, first goals. Later, you and he can add to these goals in an effort to build toward desired larger goals.

Thirty days after the initial counseling interview, meet again to jointly review progress made in the past month. Focus on accomplishments, his responsiveness to your coaching, and mutual agreement that he is beginning to discard undesirable attitudes and behaviors.

If you're not satisfied with his progress, review his future plans with him again. Ask if any modifications are necessary. Perhaps unforeseen obstacles have developed, or he has second thoughts about the agreements reached during the initial counseling interview.

Ninety days after the start of the rehabilitation program, meet again for a progress review discussion. At this interview, note your subordinate's level of enthusiasm and optimism about achieving his goals. Also, try to be sensitive to any signs that he may be regressing to former undesirable patterns of behavior and attitudes. Finally, make a judgment as to whether he is likely to make sufficient improvement in performance to merit his continued employment.

At this time, if you don't feel confident that your subordinate has responded well, or is at least starting to respond, you have no further alternative. It's time to terminate him.

TERMINATION with DIGNITY

If you've decided that an employee is not worth salvaging or that it's highly unlikely that your salvage efforts will succeed, you still have an obligation to him, the company, and yourself. Tell him that after careful consideration, you have decided to replace him. This shouldn't come as a surprise to him. Instead, it should be the natural conclusion after unsuccessful attempts to counsel, develop, revitalize, and help him.

Review briefly in what ways his performance didn't satisfy job specifications and goals you both had mutually agreed on. Although he may want to contest your conclusions, listen politely and acknowledge his point of view, but don't give the impression that your conclusions are reversible. You should have based them on what you consider to be incontestable evidence.

Direct the conversation from a review of past history to his future plans. Tell him about his termination benefits and any help you or the company can give him in getting reemployed quickly. In particular, discuss the content of the job reference you intend to give to his next employer.

Although he may become emotional, and perhaps even verbally abusive, it's vital that you not lose control of yourself. Don't placate him and don't try to blame others for your decision to terminate him. However, help him to protect his self-esteem by acknowledging mitigating circumstances and explaining that the mismatch between him and his job, work situation, and you might be avoided in the future through careful selection of his next job. In effect, the termination should be treated like an amicable divorce. The estranged partners shouldn't separate in bitterness just because their relationship didn't work out. The terminated employee's company and supervisor should cooperate in increasing the employee's personal awareness of his or her requirements for a more desirable future match.

By being helped during the termination interview to understand "what went wrong," he'll learn from the experience and not allow himself to be mismatched again.

PART TWO

Concerns
of the Individual

CHAPTER NINE

Nonpromotable
by Whose Yardstick?

You can be branded as nonpromotable prematurely by unqualified judges who use imperfect criteria and methods. You may feel that won't happen to you. You know you have talents and work hard. And in the past, you won promotions. You're confident that you'll continue your upward progress as long as you are measured by a true yardstick.

But the trueness of yardsticks is by no means a certainty. Your judges possess many feelings and predispositions that distort their readings of your capabilities. They may "like" you or "dislike" you for flimsy reasons. On a purely arbitrary basis, they may decide that you don't fit the stereotypes of the kinds of persons they consider to be promotable. To reinforce their feelings, they filter their impressions of you, seeing only what they want to see. In so doing, they deliberately or unconsciously exaggerate your weaknesses and minimize or overlook your strengths.

Besides, you'll probably be judged on what you have done, and not what you're capable of doing. Because you haven't demonstrated the qualities they seek, regardless of whether you had an opportunity to do so, you are judged not to have them. Or even if you have demonstrated qualities you'll need in higher-level jobs, they may choose to evaluate you on the basis of other qualities. With a flexible yardstick, you're as tall or short as your judges want you to be.

So it's possible, perhaps even probable, that you'll be misjudged some time in the future. And when that happens, feeling angry and complaining that you haven't been treated fairly will do you no good. Even worse, you may believe there's a simple explanation for your lack of advancement that you can't do anything about:

I had a disagreement with my boss. We both lost our tempers, and he has never forgotten it. He'll always hold a grudge against me.

When I refused to relocate and turned down a promotion, I wrecked my career. In the last 10 years there have been no other offers made to me, even though there have been many openings.

One screw-up did me in. I made a mistake that cost the company money and nobody ever forgot it.

I can't get a better job. I don't have the right credentials. Because of financial reasons, I had to drop out of college after one year and didn't complete my education. That's why I never got promoted.

But nonpromotability can rarely be explained simply. You should demand a full explanation. Perhaps you'll find sufficient grounds for an appeal. Or, at the very least, your systematic challenge will divulge information that will help rid you of disturbing feelings of having been misjudged.

JUDGES, CRITERIA, and METHODS

Rating Your Boss

The logical starting target for your challenge is your boss. He should know you better than anyone else in your company. He supervises you directly and has many opportunities in which to evaluate you. Most importantly, he appraises your performance and can recommend you for promotion.

But he may not know you as well as you think. Many things interfere with his perceptions. His competence, feelings toward you, work style, character traits, and motivations may make it virtually impossible for him to be completely fair and objective. That's why you should take a close look at him.

A rating form (see Worksheet 8) will help you to do this in a systematic way. A simple 1-to-5 scale is used for each rating, with 5 the highest rating and 1 the lowest. A rating of 3 represents the middle of the scale, neither high nor low.

WORKSHEET 8
Rating your boss.

		Strong				Weak
Competence	Education	5	4	3	2	1
	Experience	5	4	3	2	1
	Performance	5	4	3	2	1
	Leadership	5	4	3	2	1
Feelings	Openness	5	4	3	2	1
Toward You	Respectfulness	5	4	3	2	1
	Trustfulness	5	4	3	2	1
	Helpfulness	5	4	3	2	1
	Confidence	5	4	3	2	1
	Understanding	5	4	3	2	1
Workstyle	Communicativeness	5	4	3	2	1
	Energy	5	4	3	2	1
	Independence	5	4	3	2	1
	Courage	5	4	3	2	1
	Orderliness	5	4	3	2	1
Character	Calmness	5	4	3	2	1
Traits	Tolerance	5	4	3	2	1
	Genuineness	5	4	3	2	1
	Flexibility	5	4	3	2	1
	Contentment	5	4	3	2	1
Motivation	Achievement	5	4	3	2	1
	Recognition	5	4	3	2	1
	Responsibility	5	4	3	2	1
	Security	5	4	3	2	1
	Belongingness	5	4	3	2	1
	Esteem	5	4	3	2	1

The first series of ratings concerns your feelings about the competence of your boss. Is he well educated? Does he have sufficient technical education for his current responsibility? What kind of experience has he had — specialty experience as well as general supervisory experience? How long has it been since he had his specialized experience? How broad has his supervisory experience been? What is his record of performance? Is he regarded generally as a top performer? An average performer? Has his performance earned him the respect of his superiors, peers, and subordinates? Will his leadership style encourage your personal growth? Does he delegate freely? How closely does he control you? Does he advocate subordinate participation and involvement in problem solving and decision making? Is he a strong or weak leader?

The second set of ratings concerns the feelings your boss has toward you. How open is his relationship with you? Does he tell you what he thinks and what he expects? Does he level with you? Does he confide in you? Does he respect you as a person? Does he respect your skills and feelings? Does he trust you? When you make requests, does he suspect ulterior motives? Does he withhold information from you? Will he rely on your word? Is he helpful? Does he talk well of you in front of others? Does he pitch in and give you a hand when you are in trouble? Is he interested in your development? Does he back you up when you're in trouble? How much confidence does he have in you? Will he give you freedom of action? Does he entrust you with important responsibilities? Will he rely on your judgment? How understanding is he? Is he willing to listen to and accept your points of view? Does he understand your needs and motivations?

The third set of ratings concerns your boss's work style. How communicative is he? Does he communicate frequently? Does he communicate completely and accurately? Is he a good listener? How energetic is he? Does he set a good example by working harder than anybody under his supervision? Is he continually initiating new projects? How independent is he? Can he make decisions on his own? Will he maintain an unpopular point of view when under pressure? How much courage does he have? Will he take reasonable risks? Will he stand up for what he believes in? How orderly is he? Is he well organized? Does he do things systematically and thoroughly?

The fourth set of ratings applies to your boss's personality. Is he calm and relaxed? Can he control his emotions in difficult situations? How tolerant is he? Will he accept contrary points of view? Will he accept criticism? Is he genuine or a phony? Does he tell things "as they are," or does he beat around the bush? Is he manipulative or straightforward? How flexible is he? Will he change his mind? Does he permit leeway in work assignments? Will he accept reasonable excuses? How content is he with his own job? Has he progressed well and is he promotable? Is he happy with the company? Does he like the work he's doing?

The last set of ratings concerns your feelings about the boss's motivation. Is he achievement oriented? Does he have a record of accomplishment as well as a strong desire to get results? Is he more concerned with what gets done than with how it gets done? Does he set progressively more ambitious objectives for himself? Does he respond well to recognition? Is he proud of the awards and other symbols of recognition he has won? Does he seek responsibility? Will he accept new responsibilities readily? How important is security to him? Does he feel secure in his present position, or does he feel threatened? Does he play it safe, or will he go out on a limb? Does he want to be "one of the boys"? Does he need the approval of his peers? His subordinates? His superiors? How concerned is he with esteem? Is title important to him? Are the trappings of title important? Is he impressed with people who have higher status?

Besides your boss, who else has an influence in evaluating your promotability? They are your next challenge targets. You should identify each of them and their respective roles, questioning their competence, feelings toward you, work styles, character traits, and motivations.

Third-Party Judges

Everybody you work with may contribute to your evaluation—subordinates, peers, and superiors—but they don't all have equal influence. As a rule of thumb, the more status someone has, the more the weight his opinion carries.

However, status is not the only determinant of relative importance in the evaluation process. Others to whom your boss or his superior relate closely can profoundly affect your promotability. For example, one nonpromotable describes his major detractor as someone with whom he did not have a direct working relationship, but who was his neighbor:

He was a member of the general manager's personal staff and, unfortunately, his children didn't get along with mine. Their squabbles escalated into feuding between our wives and eventually, we were embroiled in it. This spilled over into the work environment and was disastrous for me. He waited for opportunities to sharpshoot, exposing my mistakes and creating company-wide doubts about my competence. I'm convinced his vote made a difference when I was being considered for promotion.

Of course, the boss's superior can be either a powerful protagonist or antagonist. His declared veto is deadly. Any unfavorable comments by him can be damaging. All he has to do is say something like any of these statements:

"I'm not certain if he is the right man."
"There's something about him that makes me uncomfortable about promoting him."
"Is he the kind of person you feel we should put into that job?"

Sometimes the burden of promotability judgments is lifted from the shoulders of your boss by the personnel staff, other designated assessors, or outside psychological consultants. These third parties supposedly bring objectivity to the assessment. For just a minisegment of a person's career, they judge him and his record. With supreme confidence, they make "yes" or "no" judgments by interpreting findings from interviews and various paper tests. Even the most determined and self-confident supervisors question their own judgment after receiving a contrary opinion from third-party specialists.

Influence of the Boss-to-Be

Another judge that can create doubts is your boss-to-be. Your current boss recommends; the boss-to-be almost always has the right to agree or disagree. Sometimes this right is exercised vigorously, after studying all objective data and conducting intensive interviews. Too often it is exercised superficially, with final judgment resting on his vague feelings. Yet the impact of that judgment extends beyond the position under consideration. The boss-to-be tries to justify his decision by reporting back damaging observations. Your boss feels embarrassed because he had not seen these "deficiencies" in you; this makes him hesitant about recommending you for future promotions.

Not only should all judges be challenged, but so should their methods. These vary from "gut feelings" to supposedly more objective data, such as intelligence and psychological tests, interviews, in-basket exercises, and simulations. All methods, depending on the competence of the judges, may provide valid data. But, a single judge using a single method is less likely to be accurate than is an assessment made by a number of judges using a variety of methods.

Regardless of which methods are used, judges often make arbitrary decisions about who is or isn't worthy of promotion. Ideally, they should compare candidate qualifications against the specifications for a specific position. They should know what they want: the total amount of pertinent experience, both technical and supervisory; education or advanced training required; evidence of managerial abilities, such as planning, organizing, motivating, delegating, developing, and controlling; mental abilities and motivation; desirable personality characteristics; any special requirements. Instead, they depend on general impressions of your capabilities. They tend to stereotype you:

"He's a goof-off."
"He's sneaky. I wouldn't turn my back on him."
"She's a woman. How can she possibly manage men?"
"He's an old-timer. What can he possibly know about modern techniques?"
"He's a mouse."
"She's unstable and immature."

The Interview

Judges are overly interested in how you present yourself in an interview. In the Big 90 (the hour-and-a-half interview is a

favorite length of time for most professional interviewers) you
may make unfavorable impressions that destroy your chances
of promotion. In business, interviewers with questionable
skills make sweeping judgments from a single interview. Yet,
in clinical interviews, psychologists rarely attempt to draw
conclusions from a single interview.

Special Tests

Just as the interview is misused as an evaluative device, so
are intelligence and psychological tests. They were not designed originally for the purpose for which they are used.
They weren't intended to provide "yes" and "no" answers
about people. They just provide data that compare your answers to test questions with those of others who have taken
the same test. Significant variations between your test scores
and group norms are treated as irrefutable evidence. Yet psychologists have waged vicious battles as to the validity of
widely used tests.

Using a combination of methods, a formal approach to
evaluating promotability evolved in the last two decades,
which resulted in the creation of the Assessment Center. The
center is based on four simple well-tested principles:

1. Many opinions are better than one.
2. People act in well-constructed simulated situations in
   the same way as they do in real life.
3. Observations in an Assessment Center environment are
   more intense than casual daily work observations.
4. There's a strong correlation between certain behavioral
   traits and subsequent managerial performance.

During a three-day period, twelve assessees are observed
by six assessors in a series of structured and unstructured simulations. They are also interviewed and take intelligence and
psychological tests. They complete in-basket exercises during
which time they respond to in-baskets full of memos, letters,
and reports. After the assessees have completed the tests and
simulations, the assessors convene as a group and prepare a
combined appraisal report to evaluate five categories of skills
—individual work characteristics, decision-making ability,

organizational and planning style, leadership behavior, and interpersonal characteristics.

The Assessment Center can provide a valuable means to evaluate one's chances for career advancement. However, it's not the final answer. It is expensive to screen large numbers of people; the quality of the appraisal report depends on the training and ability of the assessors; the glimpse of work life provided by the Assessment Center may or may not correlate with real work life, as people working under a spotlight often respond atypically; and finally, the interaction of the assessors can slant an appraisal report. One or two strong-willed, aggressive, and biased assessors may dominate timid colleagues, which distorts the appraisal report.

WHAT COUNTS against PROMOTION?

Obviously, whoever the judges and whatever their methods, subjectivity is inescapable in the evaluative process. To learn more about the degree to which subjectivity is involved, the author conducted a series of workshops in the Career Development Center of Fairleigh Dickinson University. Participants both in lower-level and higher-level jobs were asked, "Besides objective data, what else counts in promotion?"

The Lower-Level Position

For the most part, participants in lower-level positions discussed the importance of the relationship between superior and subordinate. As subordinates or people in modest supervisory positions, this group emphasized the vital role of a boss as sponsor. People he liked, he boosted upward; those he didn't like, he kept in the same job indefinitely. This group of participants covered many aspects of the superior–subordinate relationship, as discussed in the following paragraphs.

Attitude and Value Differences

According to the workshop participants, "opposites don't attract." They felt their superiors were attracted to subordinates whose attitudes and values were similar to their own. For example, orderly superiors preferred subordinates who valued orderliness;   achievement-oriented   managers   preferred achievement-oriented subordinates; intellectual managers expected their subordinates to value intellectual pursuits. For example, one young man in his first job for less than two years, told of the woes he encountered because of a basic dissimilarity between his own personality and that of his immediate superior:

All my boss ever thinks about is money. He's impressed with his big car, expensive house, and 34-foot boat. He can't understand why money is not the same turn-on for me as it is for him. The fact that I spent time in the Peace Corps immediately after college is amazing to him. He chides me for not being aggressive and complains that I'm too honest in my relationships with customers.

In my company you have to spend time in the sales force before you go into any other department. I'm concerned that his evaluation of me as a salesman is going to hurt my chances of progressing to a job that's more appropriate for me.

Past Conflicts

Many of the participants believed that their bosses didn't like subordinates who were hard to handle. They didn't go so far as to say that you had to be a "yes" man, but they felt conformity and obedience gained favors from the boss. Being outspoken usually led to trouble. All agreed that bosses had long memories that would not blot out all the gory details of past disagreements. Everybody commiserated with a young woman who long regretted confronting her boss about his work style: "Remember when you disagreed with me and gave me that business school nonsense about motivating people to assume self-control? Now do you see why I have to be so tough? If I didn't sit on top of people, they would never get their work done. There's no place for a soft manager. I was right, wasn't I?"

Competitiveness

Insecure managers, according to the group, tended to be jealous of subordinates, competing with them rather than helping them. Strong, ambitious performers were viewed as threatening to the insecure manager. Thus, achievement evoked criticism instead of praise. Managers went on the defensive because they wanted to "look better" to their subordinates. And when subordinates looked too good, they wanted to "knock them down a peg or two." Describing this kind of relationship with her manager, one woman remarked:

Nobody in my department expected our boss to go to bat for them for promotion. If she did that, she would have to admit that the successful record of the department was the result of our joint efforts. She wanted her boss and people in other departments to believe that she ran the show all by herself. We were just a bunch of flunkies who ran errands for her. How could anybody get promoted with a boss like that?

Poor Communications

Everyone at the workshops believed poor communications were a major factor in hurting the superior–subordinate relationship and in blocking promotability. Among the typical responses were:

My boss never tells me what he wants. I have to try to guess.

He's always in such a rush. He gives me partial or incomplete orders, and I make mistakes and look bad.

He forgets to pass on important information. Either he assumes I don't need the information or he gets sidetracked. Regardless of the reason, it hurts me because it affects my performance.

She never listens to me, or she listens to what she wants to hear. Many of our misunderstandings are directly related to her inattentiveness.

He rarely gives me any feedback. So I assume I'm doing the job right until I find out later, when it's too late, that I fouled up.

He throws complicated orders at me, without giving me time to fully understand them. And then he gets impatient if I ask questions or check back later. No wonder I don't follow through in the way he expected.

Whereas the group readily discussed the deficiencies of their bosses as communicators and acknowledged communication difficulties as contributing to misunderstandings and faulty performance, they appeared reluctant to discuss their own shortcomings as communicators. Drawing them out, they began to admit begrudgingly that they, too, shared the responsibility for poor communications. Their own faulty listening, speaking, and writing habits strained the superior–subordinate relationship.

Mutual Distrust

For a variety of reasons, mutual distrust may develp between superior and subordinate. As distrust grows, the psychological distance between them widens. It's impossible to feel close, understanding, and friendly toward someone you don't trust.

When asked how distrust develops, the members of the group had mixed feelings. They agreed that some people tend to be naturally "open" or "guarded," and that openness fosters trust, whereas guardedness interferes with it. Furthermore, the kind of boss who hits the ceiling when something goes wrong, or is sarcastic when criticizing mistakes, keeps his subordinates at a distance. And if either subordinate or superior feels that the other sometimes "stretches the truth," trust disappears.

The group consensus was that manipulation breeds distrust. They believed that when someone feels he's being manipulated, he'll search for "hidden agendas" in the future. In one of the workshops, a young woman expressed the feelings of the group when she said,

The first day on the job I knew I would have trouble with my boss. He was the type of person who doesn't say much, but whose mind is always churning. Whatever he did say had a bite on it, putting me on the defensive. Obviously, he was someone with whom I would have to be careful.

Some people, when you first meet them, are warm and open, and you accept them like an old friend. Others, like my boss, you know will never be your friend. He won't trust you and you won't trust him.

The Higher-Level Position

In workshops with participants in higher-level jobs, there was a dramatic shift in emphasis. This group attributed most promotability problems to subordinate deficiencies. In fact, problems in subordinate–superior relationships were discussed only lightly. Their responses focused on the major areas discussed in this section.

Lack of Drive

As one spokesman for the group said, "Although everybody claims to want to get promoted, only a select few really want it badly enough to pay the price. They just don't possess the driving ambition prerequisite to consistent, high performance."

However, they acknowledged that unrewarded driving ambition tends to sputter and fade, or it may be redirected to off-the-job activities that give greater psychological rewards. Many examples were given of talented, upward-bound individuals who mysteriously lost their drive for advancement. In each case, subsequent probing demonstrated a variety of reasons for the turn-off:

He and his wife had been battling for years, and I think he used the job to escape from her. But when he found a girlfriend, we lost him. He didn't quit, he just stopped working.

He was headed for a top job in our company, but he became impatient. He wanted advancement faster than we could give it to him. Once he mastered one job, if he wasn't already lined up for his next job, he would press hard. In the past, pressing his bosses for advancement had served him well. But when his upward mobility slowed because of a lack of promotional opportunities, his impatience became self-defeating.

Thus, although drive was judged as essential to upward mobility, it was characterized not as a constant force but one that surged or became inactivated depending on accompanying psychological rewards. Furthermore, it was often redirected to activities off the job.

Lack of Personal Growth

Responses in the area of personal growth centered around waning interest in learning and self-development. Lack of personal growth is shown in the following descriptions:

He was a top-notch engineer, but he didn't keep up to date with new developments. He didn't read much and rarely attended any outside seminars. He just never grew into the next job level.

He just didn't grow up. A lack of maturity is acceptable in a young beginner; it's intolerable in a middle manager with supervisory responsibility. He couldn't take criticism. He lost his temper over little things, and pouted if he couldn't get his way.

Personal growth was defined as continual learning and maturing and self-development. It was considered by both groups of participants to be essential to promotability.

Low Energy

The question underlying the relationship between energy and promotability was: "How hard do I work in comparison to the others I'm competing with for promotion?"

Closely related to how hard you work is the ability to sustain a high level of energy. Important questions that were raised with regard to endurance were: "Do I work hard at tasks until they are completed? Do I work hard at necessary tasks even if I am uninterested in them? Do I work as hard at those tasks I don't like as I do at the ones I do like? Do I work hard even when rewards may be delayed or not forthcoming at all?"

At first, the workshop participants described the promotable person as someone with endless energy, and the nonpromotable as an unenthusiastic worker. As the discussion continued, the images of the promotable and nonpromotable began to converge. But all agreed that over the long run the nonpromotable displayed less energy and sustained it for shorter periods of time.

Poor Work Habits

Lumped under the heading of poor work habits were a wide range of responses:

Many nonpromotables are careless about their work standards. As long as they complete a task, they don't worry about its quality. A "quick and dirty" effort often satisfies them.

They're not well organized. They often act without planning or thinking. Rarely do they set objectives and priorities. When they do, they are inappropriate.

Deadlines are ignored. Being late doesn't appear to upset them.

Many are poor problem solvers. They have difficulty understanding a problem and rush to hasty solutions before identifying the causes of problems.

Once again, the group described black-and-white differences between the promotable and the nonpromotable individual. Promotables were perceived as perfect, nonpromotables as imperfect. Gradually, this definite dichotomy evolved into the feeling that "The work habits of the promotables were usually superior to those of nonpromotables, but not always. And management preferred to believe that promotables were more efficient than nonpromotables."

Unsatisfactory Interpersonal Relationships

The idealized upward-bound subordinate was visualized as "making a good general impression; forceful without being overpowering; concerned with the feelings of people without being too soft; in full control in a conflict situation; persuasive without being manipulative . . . ." In short, the promotable was seen as a paragon of virtue. And, of course, the nonpromotable was the complete opposite. But then one dissenter spoke out: "Who are we trying to kid? We all know various successful men and women with many weaknesses and nonpromotables with many strengths. Let's be realistic."

Participants in the discussion that followed decided that upward mobility was possible regardless of flaws in interpersonal skills. However, those who had these flaws had to have "compensating strengths," such as technical competence, creativity, or extraordinary intelligence. On the other hand, the ability to get along well with others was considered helpful in improving prospects for promotability. But it was only one of many talents in the matrix for success.

Thus, the series of workshops demonstrated that regardless of job level, all participants readily acknowledged that subjective factors count heavily in determining promotability.

CHALLENGING the VERDICT

Since subjective factors affect whether or not you will be promoted, it is useful to have a systematic approach. Worksheet 9 is designed to point up practical criteria for you to review.

After recording the date, name, and title of the person who has made the appraisal, write a brief description of the circumstances associated with it. Describe the promotional opportu-

WORKSHEET 9
Challenging the justness of nonpromotability.

Date _____ Appraised by: _____	
CIRCUMSTANCES:	
RESULTS OF INTERVIEW(S):	
KEY OBJECTIONS:	
EVIDENCE	
Facts	Feelings
REBUTTAL:	
STRATEGY FOR APPEAL:	

nity and include who recommended you, the number of competitors for the opening, and any other pertinent background information. The point is that you want to get all the facts on paper so you will be equipped to analyze your next step. The examples show how one employee who was passed over for promotion completed the worksheet.

Circumstances

I was interviewed for a promising opportunity in the purchasing department. The job opening was posted officially on the personnel bulletin board. The job specification sheet listed a series of qualifications. I felt I was as qualified for the job as any of the six people who had applied for it. And I had seniority in my current job. According to company policy, my boss had to screen my application first. This concerned me because two years ago, when I had applied for another opening, had refused to submit a recommendation on the grounds that I wasn't ready for promotion.

[*Describe the interviews that led to your belief that you had been classified as nonpromotable.*]

Results of Interviews

I met with my boss and we discussed the job opening. He reviewed the job specifications with me and agreed that I met the general qualifications. However, he felt that I should not apply for the job. When I pressed him for reasons, he said my chances for getting the job were slim, and he didn't want me to feel embarrassed by a rejection. However, I insisted that I would take my chances, and he agreed to forward the application.

Subsequently, when I met with the supervisor of the new department, I was rushed through the interview and treated summarily. I had the distinct impression that I was not being given full consideration. When I confronted him, I was shown the letter of recommendation he had received from my boss. Well, it did make some positive statements about me, but strong negatives were also expressed.

[*After the interviews, you should use the worksheet to record key objections stated by the interviewers.*]

Key Objections

My boss had written, "In my opinion, he is not forceful enough to lead others. He is a pleasant, low-key person who appears to be reluctant to confront others. I suspect he may be timid. In group situations he tends to be a loner. He's never the center of attention and doesn't appear to mix well. And, he rarely makes any leadership attempts."

[*The next step is critical. You must gather the evidence against you, taking care to separate fact from feeling. In the example we are using, the boss was confronted about his unfavorable letter of recommendation; the subordinate asked his boss for further details. This is what he was told.*]

Evidence

Facts. Over the last five years I've seen you take part in about 20 sales meetings. At these meetings you tend to be much quieter than most of the other men. And in the evenings when the men get together to have a few drinks or play cards, you don't join them.

Furthermore, at several of these meetings, particularly the one I held during the last selling cycle, each time a strong disagreement arose, all you did was sit quietly and listen. Even when the men tried to get you to take sides, you backed off and remained neutral.

Feelings. The boss feels that men with leadership potential should act the way he does at sales meetings. He participates actively and forcefully and likes subordinates who do the same. He's also an intuitive decision maker and makes up his mind quickly. He attributes my slowness in decision making to indecisiveness. Also, because he likes to be one of the boys and mix with the other salesmen socially, he feels that any good leader should do likewise.

Section V of the worksheet is for *rebuttal* of the evidence that supports the key objections to your promotion. The quality of the facts should be examined. Are they accurate? Are they complete?

Examine your boss's feelings next. Do you understand them fully? Are they deep-seated or superficial?

Use the last section of the worksheet to plan a strategy for appeal. If the facts were inaccurate, an appeal would consist of an attempt to try to demonstrate the inaccuracies. If the facts were incomplete, you would have to gather additional facts and present a more complete picture of your capabilities.

Coping with inaccurate feelings is more difficult. You won't succeed in changing your boss's feelings by appealing to his logic. Instead, appeal to his emotions. For example:

Strategy for Appeal

My boss has a strong desire for the approval of his subordinates. In fact, he was quite uncomfortable when I confronted him. Knowing that his feelings play an important part in his decisions, I'll appeal to him on a personal level. I'll stress my loyalty and commitment to him of the last five years. I'll agree with his observations, as seen through his eyes, but I'll share with him my own feelings about the same events. If I can get him to understand how my feelings would cause me to act differently than he expected, it may create some doubts in his mind. Thereafter, I'll ask him, as a personal favor, to meet with the other supervisor and myself to discuss my strengths and weaknesses.

If I can't get him to change his feelings about me or his standards for promotions, I'll have to ask for a transfer or consider leaving the company.

You should not accept being branded as nonpromotable without a systematic challenge. Judges are subjective and may be unqualified, and they often make mistakes. Criteria for promotability may be arbitrary and unrealistic. Evaluation methods are imperfect and can be misleading. Therefore, it's up to you to challenge them. Otherwise, even though nonpromotability is inevitable, it could be forced on you prematurely.

CHAPTER TEN

Changing Jobs for Something Better or Escaping?

Nonpromotability often results from a job change or from too many job changes. Those most anxious to succeed sabotage themselves by becoming impatient and rushing their career progress.

The Broadway play of a decade ago, "What Makes Sammy Run," could have been dedicated to the man climbing the executive ladder. He fits the image of the ambitious man racing breathlessly ahead to seek fame and fortune. He feels his promotions never come fast enough and that job-hopping is the best way to accelerate his progress.

These breathless racers suffer from chronic cases of overconfidence complicated by self-delusions. It is a common malady that can wreck their careers and precipitate premature nonpromotability. Whereas self-confidence is important, overconfidence is dangerous and destructive. That's why you should find out if you really are a "hot shot," or whether you're just fooling yourself. Otherwise, moving up too fast—before you're ready—can create as many problems as can moving too slowly.

To give you some insights, complete Worksheet 10; then ask your boss or some of your peers (whoever you think will be most objective) to rate you.

How do you compare with your peers for each of the ten

WORKSHEET 10
Peer comparison ratings.

Better than = 3
Equal to = 2
Not as good as = 1

	3	2	1
General mental ability			
Work habits			
Energy			
Organization and planning			
Interpersonal relationships			
Stability			
Leadership			
Problem solving			
Decision making			
Self-objectivity			

characteristics? Are you smarter and more creative? How good are your work habits? Are you usually more thorough and accurate than others? Is your energy level higher? Are you better organized? Are you a more effective planner? Do your interpersonal relationships compare favorably? Do you communicate more clearly than others, both orally and in writing? Are you more adaptable — can you shift easily from situation to situation? Are you more stable, particularly under conditions of stress or uncertainty? Are you a more natural leader? Are you more independent than they, or do you usually need the approval of others? Are you a better problem solver and decision maker? How objective have you been in comparing yourself with your peers?

ESCAPING to OTHER JOBS

The grass-is-greener syndrome not only afflicts ambitious people but is equally attractive to those who want to escape from an intolerable boss, frustrating work situations, or imminent failure. Unfortunately, escape is usually temporary and the green grass turns out to be full of weeds. A chronic job-hopper has learned this lesson:

Whenever I take a new job, I feel it's the best thing that ever happened to me — and my last job is the worst. For a few months, everything is perfect. Then I start running into some of the same problems I encountered in previous jobs. By year end, I get that "oh-what-did-I-ever-take-this-job-for" feeling. And my previous job, in retrospect, looks better than it ever did. I'm on a merry-go-round that's taking me nowhere fast.

Even those who change jobs successfully learn, after several job changes, that opportunity and risk go hand in hand. Each new job makes new demands, sometimes beyond their capabilities. In fact, according to some leading career-development experts, 25 percent of managers who leave one company for a higher-level position in another company fail in the new position. When I asked for an explanation of this startling statistic, here's what I was told:

Succeeding in a new job depends on more than just personal competence. Other critical factors are the nature of the assignment, the work environment, and most importantly, the new boss. I've seen many men fail because they took on impossible assignments at which nobody had a chance to succeed. Or they went to work for a company with restrictive policies and procedures that stymied them, as well as hostile in-groups that continually undermined them. And, unfortunately, many find that the smiling men who interviewed them become miserable SOB's who delight in harassing, belittling, and destroying them.

EVALUATING YOUR CURRENT JOB

There are considerable risks involved in changing jobs, so before you consider this big step, evaluate your current job. Here are some important questions you should ask yourself, with an example for each group to help you sharpen your focus.

How long have I been in my current job? What has been the average time required to qualify for advancement in my department and in other departments? Are there any young men in higher-level jobs, or are they aging relics gathering dust?

> My boss has been in the same job for ten years and he won't retire for twenty years. Since there are virtually no interdepartmental promotions in my company, I feel dead-ended.

Are you as satisfied with your job now as you were when you joined the company? To what extent have your expectations been realized? In what ways have you been disappointed? What promises haven't been fulfilled?

> I was told my job would be challenging, but it's become routine. I'm not learning new skills, and I don't use my full talents.

Are you satisfied with your personal growth? Has your salary progressed well? How does it compare with the salaries received by others in similar jobs inside and outside the company? Have you been given increased responsibilities?

> Although I am responsible for more important things than when I first started this job, my salary has not kept up with my increasing responsibilities. I've been getting salary increases at the rate of 5 percent annually. Everybody around here gets the same size raise whether they do a good or bad job. So although I started with a decent wage, it's now below the industry average.

If you perform well, what career opportunities are available to you? Do you project few or many openings in the near future?

> There are many job opportunities in my company. The speed at which we're growing creates new openings all the time. And

the company believes in promoting from within. Also, there's considerable intracompany job mobility—you can jump from department to department.

How strong is the competition for future job openings? Are many qualified people available for each opening? How do you rank among candidates for promotion?

I'm working with a sharp bunch of men and women. They're well educated and have good experience. It's tough to pull ahead of the pack. I'm beginning to wonder if I'd be better off in another company where there's less competition.

Are you ready for, or getting ready for, promotion? Are you getting adequate training and development—formal and informal—on the job?

My boss is highly qualified and I can learn much from him. Furthermore, he takes an interest in my development. He delegates freely and controls lightly. The company encourages its employees to develop themselves. They pay for externally sponsored courses and provide in-company training.

What is your relationship with your boss? Is he a protractor or a detractor? Does he respect you? Does he want you to succeed?

My boss holds me back. He's forever belittling me. He never gives me credit. And he rarely gives me anything worthwhile to do. I know he doesn't give a damn about me.

What is the reputation and influence of your boss and your department? Do he and your department have high visibility within the organization?

My boss is the golden boy of the company. Everybody asks for his advice and listens to him. The people in my department benefit from his influence. We're treated with respect and are considered to be professionals. I'm really lucky to be working for him in this department.

How much freedom of action and job discretion do you have? Can you make many of your own decisions? Can you do things in your own way? Can you use initiative?

I'm having a ball working in my present job. Although my boss approves my goals and budgets, how I reach those goals is my business. He doesn't butt in unless I'm doing something that violates company policy.

What has been your record of achievement? Have you solved difficult problems? Have you produced outstanding results?

For the last three years, all the brands I have managed have shown sharp sales gains and profits. Yet we faced strong competitive challenges and major cost increases.

What's your image in the department and the company? Is it favorable or unfavorable? Are you stereotyped?

I'm called "old reliable." Everybody respects me and believes I'm dependable. But they see me as a staff type. So when line opportunities occur, nobody expects me to throw my hat in the ring.

How much good or bad will, or both, have you accumulated? Who are your friends and your enemies?

I'm well liked by everybody. I have strong supporters in my own department and in other departments. I know that when I become a candidate for promotion, I'll have many people rooting for me.

Are you ready to make the transition from technical specialist to generalist? Do you know how to get work done through people? Are you a leader? What opportunities have you had to find out about your managerial potential?

This is really a progressive company. I attended an assessment center and was given feedback on my ability to work with people and assume leadership. On several occasions, I participated in T groups in which I gained insights into my interpersonal effectiveness. I've also served as a task force leader. In that capacity, without any formal authority, I had to get the other members of the task force to work with me to get a job accomplished.

Are you thinking in terms of the short or long range about your career? How willing are you to wait to fulfill your wants and needs?

I need more money now. So I'm trying to decide if I should go to another company where I can make more money immediately even though I know my future here is good.

What's the key to advancement in your current position? Is it influence, seniority, or merit? Will good performance automatically qualify you for promotion?

This company is highly political. It's not what I do that counts — it's who I know. I've watched some guys who are far less qualified than I am win quick promotions because they had good connections.

Have you overlooked anything in evaluating your current job? Whom should you ask to check your conclusions? Can they be trusted? Do they agree or disagree with you?

I had decided that my current job just wasn't for me. But then I had a long talk with my wife and with a close friend in another department. Both gave me different perspectives. I realized I was temporarily depressed and frustrated. That was no reason to change jobs.

Now that you've evaluated your current job, you may feel it's unlikely that you will be promoted in the foreseeable future. But you are confident that you are ready for promotion and deserve one. While you're in a job-changing frame of mind, the phone rings:

I'm a management recruiter searching for a marketing director candidate for a well-known company in your industry. Do you know of somebody who might qualify for this job?"

Oh! It sounds like a good job. What does it pay? I might be interested myself.

And so the courtship begins. Unfortunately, it's usually a whirlwind courtship and you find yourself married before you really know much about your mate. This is a very precarious practice. Changing jobs without thoroughly investigating a new job opportunity can hurt your career.

To avoid this danger, make a thorough side-by-side comparison of your current job and your new job using the form shown in Worksheet 11.

Is the growth of the new company better or worse than that of your current company? The faster its rate of growth, the more likely job opportunities will be available in the future.

WORKSHEET 11
Comparison of current and new jobs.

CHARACTERISTIC	BETTER	WORSE	DON'T KNOW
Company growth	___	___	___
Company reputation	___	___	___
Company structure	___	___	___
Company policies and procedures	___	___	___
Department reputation and influence	___	___	___
Department supervision	___	___	___
Salary and benefits	___	___	___
Working conditions	___	___	___
Peer relationships	___	___	___
Job status	___	___	___
Security	___	___	___
Turnover rate	___	___	___
Responsibility	___	___	___
Advancement opportunities	___	___	___
Learning opportunities	___	___	___
Challenge	___	___	___
Variety	___	___	___
Discretion	___	___	___
Degree of stress	___	___	___
Risks	___	___	___

However, the new company may be experiencing rapid growth because of temporary conditions that could change suddenly. Or the fast growth may tax the capital structure of the company, making it financially unstable.

As a competitor, you may know much about the company or at least where to get information. Sometimes you can find out by directly questioning interviewers. Often, a good source of information about a company is a financial analyst.

What is the company's reputation? What do suppliers and customers think about the company? Is it the kind of company you would be proud to work for? Does it have a reputation for being technologically advanced and for producing high-quality, innovative products?

What is the structure of the company? Is it highly structured with many specialized departments? Will the structure allow you to interact freely with other departments? Will it be easier to become more visible in the new company than in the one you work for? To make structural comparisons, get a copy of its table of organization and compare it with the table of organization of your own company.

How do the policies and procedures of the new company compare with those of your current company? Are there many more policies and procedures, which might constrain your freedom of action? Are there any noticable differences, favorable or unfavorable? By studying the procedures manual you can learn much about it. However, don't draw conclusions based on the manual alone. Find out whether policies and procedures are followed strictly. Is it common practice to circumvent them? If it is, why is it necessary to do so? Why haven't they been rewritten?

What is the reputation and influence of the new department in which you will be working? Is it an important profit center? What kind of person is running the department? Is he well qualified? Is he respected by others in the company? How does he treat his employees? You can get information about the department by talking to current employees or, if you can locate them, past employees. Suppliers can also provide valuable insights.

How do the salary and benefits compare? Ask the personnel department for the upper and lower salary limits of your future career steps. If this is private information, ask for a relative compensation comparison. Some industries provide executive compensation surveys, which will supply this information.

How do working conditions compare? Is it noisier? More crowded? What special facilities are available? What kinds of special equipment, such as access to computer terminals, and so forth, are available?

How well do people get along with one another? Once again, discussions with present and former employees can be very revealing. Do there appear to be any rivalries? Is there any sign of departmental conflict?

What status will your new job have? You may assume it's a higher title than your present position, yet it may not give you any more status than you have currently. Titles are often misleading. For example, in some companies a group product manager may have much more authority than someone who is called a marketing director in another company.

How much security will you have in the new job? Is the reason for the increase in salary and title because the company has difficulty finding people? Is it the kind of place that has a high turnover? Find out how long most people stay with the company. Do the veterans have only one or two years' longevity?

Will your new job represent a dramatic increase in responsibility? Is it possible that the increase in responsibility is more than you can handle?

Which company offers the most opportunity to grow? On what do you base your judgment of the relative opportunities in the two companies?

How stimulating will your new job be? Will it offer a genuine challenge? Will it provide assignment variety? How much discretion will you have in selecting what you do and how you do it?

How much more pressure will you have in the new job? Will it be a high-pressure job? Will you have to deal with tight deadlines, overtime demands, and an accelerated work pace? Do you feel you'll be able to function effectively in a more stressful environment?

Finally, what do you risk by taking a new job? What do you lose and what do you gain? Is the risk of starting over again in a new, unknown situation worth the benefits that you feel you will reap in return?

Realizing the amount of time and effort it takes to compile this information, you may feel:

> I don't have forever to make up my mind about taking a new job. Besides, I don't want potential new employers to feel I don't have confidence in them. If my first impressions are good, and what they tell me sounds reasonable, I don't see why I can't make up my mind immediately.

It's a paradox that someone who applies for a new job will allow himself or herself to be subjected to multiple interviews, psychological tests, reference checks, and yet doesn't try to be as thorough in his or her own investigation of a potential employer. Why shouldn't you know as much about them as they want to know about you? You have more to lose as an individual than they have to lose as a company. If they make a mistake, you may cause them some temporary problems; if you make a mistake, you may find yourself out of work with a bad reference and poor future career prospects.

INTERNAL JOB CHANGES

Changing jobs within your company can be just as hazardous as jumping to another company. Certainly a side-by-side comparison of the current and new job will help you to make an intelligent decision. Most of the items in Worksheet 11 apply in this situation.

Of particular importance is your potential boss. As you already work within the company, it should be easy to get a fix on his personality and work style. How well liked is he by the people who work for him? Is he a demanding boss? You can minimize the dangers of changing jobs by thoroughly investigating your future boss. Yet, time after time, people foolishly put themselves under the control of a tyrant or an incompetent.

Another major problem is relocation. You may be willing to move anywhere for a promotion, but your family may feel otherwise. Actually, the hardship of relocating is greatest on the family. You may be leaving behind friends, relatives, and a community you enjoyed, but you serve to gain benefits from the new job. In contrast, the benefits gained by your family are only minimal and moving can be extraordinarily upsetting to them. Even when they look forward to the move, if things don't live up to their expectations, your household can become very unhappy.

One important consideration in any relocation is the possibility that it may take you out of the mainstream of the company. This is particularly true when someone is moving from the home office to a remote plant. Visibility fades with distance. It's very easy to become forgotten in the hinterlands.

Frequently an intracompany job change will involve dramatic differences in your responsibilities, the nature of your work, and what's expected of you. You may have to give up work activities you enjoyed and did well for activities you don't like and don't do well. This often happens to the specialist who moves up to a supervisory position. For example, a research chemist in a major oil company became the administrative head of a research department in another division. He describes what happened to him:

After years of being responsible for nobody but myself, I was really looking forward to the new assignment. It wasn't just the boost in salary or the recognition — it was the challenge of running a department in the way I thought it should be run. I had strong feelings on how a research department should be managed.

Unfortunately, I didn't have either the experience or education to do the job and there wasn't time to learn. I was the boss and everybody expected me to know what to do. But that didn't stop me from plunging into the job and making drastic changes.

As you would expect, I did some stupid things, including mishandling my subordinates. My approach was simplistic: I give the orders and they carry them out. In less than a year three valuable senior chemists quit and the rest of the department was in revolt. They issued an ultimatum to top management: Either I go, or they go. Guess who got the ax?

Even when you're fully qualified for a new job and are assuming desirable responsibilities, a series of rapid promotions can throw you off balance. That's because you don't stay on a job long enough to accumulate friends and supporters. Unfamiliar faces and unfamiliar surroundings, as well as the discomfort of being an outsider, can make your work environment unbearable.

Most people need a psychological breather between jobs. Proving yourself and reproving yourself takes a lot out of you. Until you master new responsibilities and feel accepted by your new boss and peers, it's natural to feel "uptight." Victims of the new-man-on-the-job syndrome often sound like this:

In the first few months, I set a burning work pace — 60 to 70 hours a week. I was anxious to show dramatic results. The people I worked with admired my energy, but they didn't like my methods. I knew I was stepping on toes, but I felt that after I had solved the major problems facing me, I could backtrack and mend some fences.

My impatience to prove myself as quickly as possible prolonged the usual length of time it takes for an outsider to be accepted by a new group. Other than the initial perfunctory attempts at friendship, my colleagues kept their distance. I ate lunch by myself and no one dropped around my office for small talk.

As I was living in a hotel room waiting for my family to join me when our house was sold and the school year ended, I had nothing to do in the evenings except more of what I had been doing all day long — work. And weekends in a strange place without family and friends were hell.

Besides the wear and tear of the climb upward, promotion seekers often race onto the wrong career paths. They accept promotions that give them increased status and salary, but which are not logical next career steps. In fact, they may be missteps in the wrong direction. The jobs they accept don't take advantage of their past experience and natural skills. Or they don't provide learning opportunities to help them prepare for other career steps. And although a new job appears to be a title improvement, its scope may be narrower than the previous one. For example, a new boss may want to hog responsibilities and treat you like an "assistant to." Or you may become too specialized instead of becoming a generalist.

FANTASIES of ESCAPING NONPROMOTABILITY

Job-changing for the purpose of escaping nonpromotability can worsen your situation. When things aren't going well on your present job, it's natural to think of quitting. You feel a fresh start will change your luck.

But is it bad luck, or did you cause your past problems? Do you find yourself replaying the same scenario? Here are three typical scenes from life stories that may sound familiar.

One step ahead of failure often characterizes the work history of men or women who are good at selling themselves but who don't perform as well. Their careers are marked by repeated failures. They start new jobs full of self-confidence. But eventually a combination of mounting problems and bad decisions catches up with them. Then they change jobs to escape blame for failures, leaving a mess for someone else to clean up. This scenario may be repeated numerous times until even the most glib job-hoppers find it impossible to alibi their past records.

Another escape scenario stars a bad actor with personality defects. Whatever the personality problem is — be it boastfulness, irascibility, immaturity — the afflicted person is blind to his defects. The same problems reoccur on each job. Yet he blames the job, company, or co-workers. His blindness to himself dooms him to replay the same story with the bad ending.

The third familiar story is that of the fantasizer who changes jobs dreaming of reaching top jobs. These people may be top performers in their current jobs. Unfortunately, they don't have the qualifications for promotion. So, every two or three years, sacrificing longevity and benefits and disrupting themselves and their families, they change jobs: "I know the next job will be different. They'll recognize my talents. They'll see me as I see me — someone with unlimited potential."

All of these scenarios involve a leading character who deludes himself. He refuses to look at himself in the mirror and see reality.

Instead of running away, the nonpromotable must eventually say to himself, "Wait! I don't want to punish myself anymore. I want to learn how to be happy in my present job." Before this can happen, he has to see himself as others see him. Taking time to complete the following sentences could be a helpful start:

It's hard for me to admit that_____

_____

_____

I may be causing some of my present job difficulties by___

_____

_____

I'm fooling myself by_____

_____

_____

Things may not be different in a new job because_____

_____

_____

Things may be much worse in a new job because_____

_____

_____

Things I do over and over again that are hurting me are___

_____

_____

_____

Here are typical sentence-completion responses from men and women I have counseled at the Career Development Center:

It's hard for me to admit that:
   I don't have leadership ability.
   I've changed jobs for emotional, not rational, reasons.
   I wasn't robbed of promotions — I just didn't deserve them.
   I'm not Superman.
   I haven't accepted responsibility for my career.

I may be causing some of my present job difficulties by:
Fighting authority, instead of collaborating with them.
Ignoring my shortcomings.
Being defensive and distrusting.
Not knowing how to ask for help.
Not learning how to help myself.

I'm fooling myself by:
Blaming my boss and company for my current career problems.
Doing a minimally acceptable job and punishing the company for not promoting me.
Believing I'm much better than people in my department who have been promoted.
Convincing myself that I'm promotable, regardless of strong opinions of others to the contrary.
Thinking I won't be happy unless I get promoted.

Things may not be different in a new job because:
I probably won't change.
I've been responsible for creating many of my own problems.
I'll face strong competition for promotion wherever I work.
My expectations are unrealistic.
My own attitudes are defeating me.

Things may be much worse in a new job because:
I won't have the friends and good will I've gained over the years in my present job.
I may not like my new boss, company, or the work itself.
I'm giving up seniority and many benefits associated with it.
I'll probably take it without checking it out thoroughly.

Things I do over and over again that are hurting me are:
I don't think about or plan my career.
I don't help myself to improve my job situation.
I've insatiable wants.
I ignore my own shortcomings.
I don't accept constructive criticism.

You will probably make four to seven job changes in your career. Each may strengthen or weaken your promotability. So don't make job changes impetuously, chasing fantasies or running away from unpleasant situations. Compare your present job with the new one, and change only for an opportunity you're convinced is genuinely better.

CHAPTER ELEVEN

Becoming a "Lifer"

For many individuals, mastery of their job leads to complacency, increasing boredom, and a psychological letdown. Combine the attitude that your job holds no surprises and that you can do it blindfolded with the prospect of being stuck in that job for the rest of your work career, and there's a high probability that you will develop the work habits and attitudes of the "lifer."

Look around you and you'll see many of these lifers. They're the nine-to-fivers, putting in their time and watching the clock. They don't look forward to a day's work, and the minute they leave at 5 o'clock, a mental trap door closes that doesn't reopen until 9 o'clock the next morning. They don't feel stimulated by their job or take pride in their work. And when they talk to their wives and friends about their job, more often than not, they gripe about the boss, the company, the policies, and procedures. The only reason they stay in the same job is they have no place else to go. They're locked into the company and are fearful of sacrificing benefits they have accumulated over the years. Or, in some cases, they have tried to change jobs but have been unsuccessful at finding anything better.

In workshop settings in which I described the plight of the lifer, virtually everyone knew examples of such people. But they didn't believe it could happen to them. Typically, they responded defensively, saying, "I'm not a lifer! Sure, I've been in the same job for a long time, but I know I haven't changed. I still work hard and put in long hours." As the discussion developed, some acknowledged subtle attitude changes: "I don't feel about my job the way I did when I first started working at it. It's natural, once you know the ropes, to coast a bit. Perhaps my job is not as important to me as it used to be. However, I'm older and I have many more outside interests. I've learned there's more to life than just work."

What is not well recognized is that there are critical differences in motivating factors between promotables and nonpromotables. A glance at Figure 9 shows why promotables tend to be more strongly motivated than are nonpromotables.

FIGURE 9
Critical differences in motivating factors between promotables and nonpromotables.

MOTIVATING FACTORS	PROMOTABLES	NONPROMOTABLES
Rewards	Growing	Plateauing
Status	Increasing	Decreasing
Attention	Continuing	Fading
Challenge	Increasing	Decreasing
Variety	Increasing	Decreasing
Learning opportunity	Increasing	Decreasing
Security	Increasing	Decreasing

For example, the man or woman who's promoted regularly earns more money and benefits than does someone who stays in the same job. A 20-percent-or-greater salary increase for each promotion is generally the rule in contrast with the 5 percent annual increase of those who aren't moving ahead. It's upsetting when you realize that colleagues who have the same longevity as you are earning much higher salaries.

Not only do the promotables get more money—they enjoy growing status. They get the big offices with carpeting on the floor and luxurious furnishings. They also get treated preferentially. Their opinions carry more weight. And those around them have to show more deference to them. They're also showered with attention. Because they're important to the corporation their happiness and well being are given special consideration. The corporation can't afford to lose their heirs to key jobs.

Resentful of these corporate elite, the less privileged nonpromotables feel: "Why should they get special treatment? I work just as hard, if not harder. And although I may be lower in the corporate hierarchy, I, too, have important responsibilities. Regardless of the fact that my career has run into a brick wall, I still have feelings and needs. I don't like to be ignored. I need words of praise and attention."

It shouldn't matter if you're paid less than those who are obviously getting ahead, even if you do feel ignored and neglected, as long as you enjoy the job itself. But many nonpromotables don't. How can your job be as challenging as it was in the past when much of it has become routine? You've done it all before. You don't have increasing responsibilities to stretch your capacity—to get the most out of you. You won't get a chance to work with new people and do new things.

"I'm bored to hell," said one man trapped in the same job for 10 years. He described to me the monotony of his daily routine:

For 10 years now I've been a production planner. Every day I check what's been sold and what we've produced. I make sure that inventories are maintained at prescribed levels and issue a standard report. Unless there's a screw-up, I never hear from anybody. And even then, things don't get too exciting. All I'm expected to do is help pin the tail on the donkey—find out why our stocks are too low or too high. The computer has assumed more and more of my job, and I have even less to do now than I used to. Now, instead of sorting a bunch of papers and making calculations myself, I read video displays. Otherwise, it's business as usual.

Another motivating factor that's sadly missing in the work life of the nonpromotable is satisfying learning opportunities. While the promotables attend intercompany workshops and prestigious programs outside the company, the nonpromotable must depend on his own resources to keep up to date and sharpen his skills. Besides, even if he is successful at self-development, he gets minimal opportunities to use new knowledge. Whatever he learns is soon forgotten.

Understandably, the nonpromotable feels frustrated and insecure. He begins to wonder, "Maybe management's trying to tell me something. My salary's flattening, my status is declining, I get less attention, I'm not being challenged or given new things to do, and I've stopped learning. Where is this all leading? I'm sliding backward rapidly. Will I eventually become so unimportant that I'll no longer be wanted at all? Is this the beginning of a one-way trip out of this company?"

EFFECTS of NONPROMOTABILITY

Working in an environment that is becoming increasingly demotivating changes you. At first the transformation can be almost imperceptible; in time, however, you feel, "What's the use of fighting any longer." You succumb and begin to exhibit self-destructive changes.

The typical response to nonpromotability is a wasting away of important characteristics that have contributed to your past personal successes. Your productivity, satisfaction, and temperament deteriorate progressively. All nonpromotables are affected in this way to some extent, and in predictable ways.

Decreased Productivity

Initially, you begin to lose interest in your job. And why not? It's become old hat; it's less rewarding and less challenging. This loss of interest is manifested as a growing indifference and the feeling, "I wish I had something different to do once in awhile."

Waning interest depletes your energy. You're not working as hard as you used to, and it's much more difficult to stay with tasks to completion. You're easily distracted and tend to put off things you don't like to do. If you have been a work horse all along, the change in your energy and endurance is unnoticed. But there is a definite decline in your work output. Eventually, boredom and growing indifference will also affect the quality of your work.

Declining Satisfaction

Because your aspirations have been thwarted, your morale plummets. Boredom, frustration, disillusionment, and indifference destroy your job satisfaction. You feel alienated and detached.

In a counseling interview, a victim of the nonpromotability blues said, "I don't feel like I belong here any more. Everybody else has something to look forward to. They work hard knowing they'll get a fair return for their efforts. If I work hard, all I get is to keep my job. How can I possibly be happy when I'm playing in a game where my hits don't count, and everybody makes a big deal about my errors and strike-outs?"

Poor morale robs you of your competence, drive, and creativity. Because you feel dissatisfied and unhappy, you "don't give a damn" about how well you do the job. You don't try to keep up to date and so you become obsolete. Your skills become dulled by your half-hearted approach and you do only what is minimally expected of you. In the past you actively sought responsibility; now you try to evade it. Without adequate motivation, there's no reason to drive yourself. You feel all you should give the company is an acceptable performance.

Change in Temperament

Finally, as your productivity slips and your dissatisfaction mounts, a frightening thing happens. Your temperament changes both on and off the job.

Let's examine these important changes in you as seen through the eyes of your boss, peers, friends, and relatives.

What the Boss Sees

For some time I knew something was wrong. George's performance had become uninspired and unimaginative. I knew he was capable of much more. He seemed to have lost his zest for the job. He gave up too easily on hard tasks and came running to me with problems. That wasn't like him. Also, I began to suspect him of buck-passing. And for the first time since I worked with him, he was late for deadlines.

I thought it was a temporary thing and that he'd get over it, so I didn't say anything. But then his personality began to change. He used to be a pleasure to work with. He volunteered to do things, he took criticism well, he rarely became angry, and he was a nice guy. Now he's irritable and argumentative. He over-reacts to the smallest problems. And if I am mildly critical, he becomes defensive. He's obviously unhappy. We used to horse around with each other. I'd tease him and he'd tease me. But now he rarely cracks a smile. He turned sour not only on the outside, but on the inside.

As Seen by Peers
I don't like the new George as well as I liked the old one. He used to be an enthusiastic guy who was fun to work with. Very few things bothered him and I rarely heard him bitch about the boss or the company. He would often pitch in and help other people and seemed to have an unlimited capacity for work.

Now, he has become touchy and cynical. He's continually grip-ing. He harps about "the good old days," and he's developed into a washroom lawyer, wasting his energy fighting the com-pany system rather than doing his job. What surprises me most is the fact that he's become a goof-off. He lingers at coffee breaks, takes long lunch hours, does a lot of office socializing, and is one of the first people out of the office at the end of the day.

As Seen by Friends and Relatives
Unhappiness at work tends to spill over at home. Feelings you can't let out in the office because they'll jeopardize your job are unloaded on innocent members of your family and friends. They don't know why they've become targets, and respond by fighting back. Thus, your relationships with them become strained. Here's how they view the new you:

George has become impossible to live with. He's grumpy and has developed a hair-trigger temper. Nothing pleases him and very few things interest him. He used to get great joy out of just spending time with the family or relaxing with friends. And he was active in church and community affairs. Now, when he comes home from the office, usually a lot earlier than he ever did before, he seems to be exhausted and complains he's too tired to do anything. I know it's got something to do with work, but he refuses to talk about it. It's bad now, but I'm concerned it may get worse.

Fortunately, all nonpromotables do not become "lifers" who exhibit the dramatic changes in productivity, satisfaction, and temperament that have been described. However, all to varying degrees are affected by the impact of nonpromotability.

At Fairleigh Dickinson workshops, I asked a wide cross section of men and women, "What percentage of the people you believe to be nonpromotable in your company are lifers? Indicate whether they are confirmed lifers, possible lifers, becoming lifers, definitely not lifers, or whether you're uncertain as to their status. In designating this percentage, round it off to the nearest 5 percent."

In this informal survey of more than 100 men and women representing 20 different companies, the answers were surprising and disconcerting:

Confirmed Lifers	10%
Possible Lifers	15%
Becoming Lifers	25%
Definitely Not Lifers	30%
Uncertain	20%

They identified as many as 50 percent of the nonpromotables as exhibiting dramatic changes in productivity, satisfaction, and temperament associated with being a lifer.

I asked the workshop participants a second important question: "Of the people you have identified as either being confirmed lifers, possible lifers, or becoming lifers, what percentage of them do you think understand what's happening to them? Indicate whether these people are definitely not aware, probably not aware, or whether you're uncertain of their degree of awareness. Round off the percentages to the nearest 5 percent."

The answers, if they are representative of all lifers in industry, demonstrate a serious situation:

Definitely Not Aware	15%
Probably Not Aware	25%
Possibly Not Aware	20%
Definitely Aware	20%
Uncertain	20%

According to the people surveyed, an alarming percentage of lifers are not aware or only partially aware of the harmful changes that have affected them.

RECOGNITION "BLINDERS"

Nonawareness of becoming a lifer is painfully apparent in the following exit interview dialog described by a vice president in charge of administration of a major company:

Manager: Are you trying to tell me that you don't think your work has slipped in the last two years and your attitudes haven't changed?

Subordinate: No! I believe I've been giving you a fair day's work. I may not be the best worker in the department, but I work as hard as everybody else.

Manager: But you have been late with many of your reports. And on more than a few occasions, they have been inaccurate or incomplete.

Subordinate: I just can't seem to please you.

[*Manager and subordinate argued about standards of quality, but no agreement was reached.*]

Manager: O.K., even if you don't agree with me, I still feel that your work hasn't met my expectations and that it has slipped in the last two years. Let's talk about some changes in your attitudes.

Subordinate: What changes?

Manager: I mean your attitude about your job, the company, and me. It appears to me that you used to have much more favorable attitudes.

Subordinate: I feel about the same way about my job, the company, and you as I always have. Of course, I haven't liked the idea that I've been stuck in the same job for such a long time. And I've been passed over for promotion and have only gotten

token salary increases. But I haven't let that affect me. I felt
eventually I'd get proper recognition. In fact, when you called
me in here I thought you were going to talk to me about promotion — not to tell me that I'm being fired.

How could someone be so blind to his boss's feelings about
his performance? Surely this must be an extraordinary case.
Unfortunately, it's all too common. People are surprised when
told they're being fired. Obviously, they have blinded themselves to what was happening to them and to their performance.

Recognition blinders (that is, fantasy, rationalization, aggression, fixation, internalization, and regression) hide developing crises from those who find it difficult to accept a future
that holds no upward mobility. Although these defense mechanisms offer some measure of short-term comfort and are natural reactions, their long-term consequences are dire.

Fantasy. Consider fantasy. Who doesn't daydream and hope
that "things will get better"? But fantasies have a way of getting out of hand. When you think you can wish away reality,
you're headed for trouble. That's what happened when a training manager with ten years in the same job convinced himself
that someday he would become a top line manager within his
company. He reasoned that because he was responsible for
the development of future managers, he could function in a
top-level job better than they. Acting out that fantasy, he com-
peted with managers in his training classes. He put them
down when they were awkward in handling new skills and
showed off how well he had mastered the same skills.

Taking advantage of his authority as an instructor, he pom-
pously criticized the company's line managers and boasted
how he could do much better.

Because he was an effective instructor, his actions were
tolerated. Fortunately for him, most of the managers who attended his classes didn't take his fantasies seriously. They
believed his boasting and put-downs were used deliberately
to impress them with the importance of the subject matter.

Over the years, he became even more absorbed with his
own fantasies and began to rush his advancement. Believing
he was better than the managers that attended his classes, he

tried to convince top management that he could play a major role in the company. He became more provocative in his classroom attacks and eventually reached top management. At which point they fired him!

Rationalization. To cope with his failure to advance in the company, the training manager resorted to fantasizing. Another recognition blinder is rationalization. Instead of protecting yourself with fantasy, you try to explain away your lack of advancement: "It's not my fault. Others are to blame."

You can think of good reasons for everything that has gone wrong in your career. For example, an expert at rationalization is the personnel manager in a large company that had created a department of organizational development to assume responsibilities he had shirked. He claimed he wasn't given the freedom of action to perform the function properly. He also blamed top management for withholding funds in the past and denying requests for additional staff. Of course he ignored the fact that he hadn't made any formal proposals for extra money and staff. Nor had he shown how the investment would benefit the company. He won't admit he had simply "missed the boat." He hadn't anticipated the needs of the company or developed his own skills to fill that need. As long as he continues to focus on explaining away what happened and blaming others for the dead end that he had personally constructed, he'll suffer with increasing intensity the full effects of nonpromotability.

Aggression. Some nonpromotables become blinded with rage. Such individuals are filled with anger because their careers have fizzed out. They'd rather fight reality than accept it.

A veteran engineer who has spent 20 years working in project teams has allowed anger to turn him into a lifer, as the following case illustrates.

Engineers often shift from project to project, sometimes serving as project leaders and sometimes as members of project teams. Many engineers spend their entire careers working in this fashion. A relatively small number of exceptional engineers break out of the project teams and assume managerial responsibilities. The majority don't.

For those engineers who aspire to management, the short stints as project leaders serve to whet their appetites. In this case, the aggressive lifer under discussion developed an insatiable hunger for management. He tried to prolong his tours of duty as project leader. When not assigned as a group leader, he fought the leader's authority. Furthermore, when he was interviewed for promotion and was rejected, he persisted in appealing the decisions. He became argumentative and disagreed with the explanations for his rejection. He became vindictive with "all the fools who didn't recognize his talents."

Because of his actions, he was no longer put in charge of project teams and was rarely chosen willingly by anybody to serve on their teams. In fact, he had succeeded in alienating and isolating himself. He didn't like the company or its people and he made certain that they didn't like him. By fighting nonpromotability, he had hurt himself. Thus, he created a self-fulfilled prophesy.

Fixation. Another blinder that interferes with acceptance and adjustment to reality is fixation — remaining in an immature stage of development. Psychologists think of fixation as the "arresting of one or more phases of development at a childhood or adolescent level." Under normal circumstances, we develop progressively in all respects — intellectually, emotionally, and socially. Although this process is not always smooth, we become increasingly capable of meeting different types of situations.

Normally, the person who recognizes that he or she has become nonpromotable is initially upset, but eventually learns how to live with it. In contrast, if you become fixated, you keep replaying in your mind the details of your work history, trying to find where you went wrong. This preoccupation with the past interferes with your future development.

For example, a middle-aged supervisor in the laboratory of a large hospital became a lifer because she could not accept nonpromotability. More than 20 years ago she had decided to become a laboratory technologist. She had felt that because a large proportion of the employees in hospital laboratories were women, she could compete more equally than in industry. She worked hard to become technically competent and in the evenings earned an advance degree that would make her more promotable. After several years as a technologist, she was promoted to the position of supervisor. Her career has stalled in that capacity even though she has changed jobs three times searching for a more favorable environment.

She keeps telling herself that she deserves a higher-level position in the laboratory. She's obsessed with that idea. It affects her relationship with her subordinates, her peers, and her superiors. She harps on her past mistakes, reliving each one. This tendency immobilizes her. Because she's afraid to make new mistakes, she's forever checking with her boss to see if she is doing things to his satisfaction. For the same reason, she continually rechecks her own work and that of her subordinates. This reduces the quantity of work she produces and has given her an image of a perfectionist: "She drives everybody in the lab nuts."

Internalization. Replaying the past blinds the fixated lifer; swallowing it whole has the same effect. The nonpromotable who internalizes past defeats seems adjusted to them. However, inwardly he's still troubled. Thus, he suffers from all the effects of nonpromotability, and his productivity and job satisfaction decline. But the changes in his temperament are more subdued. He appears to be the same person he has always been, but with one major difference—he's plagued by an assortment of physical aches and pains.

The personal physician of a forty-year-old product manager describes his patient as follows:

He's a regular! Every year I see him about six times. Most often, he's suffering from a gut problem, but he has complained of a variety of other problems. His patient history record is cluttered with notations that catalog the vague symptoms he has suffered over the years. After a routine examination I ask him, "How are things going for you?" Automatically he starts telling me about work: "Things are going well, but . . . ." Obviously he's concerned about his lack of progress on the job. But he has never said so directly. I'm sure I'm one of the few people to whom he has confided at all. Evidently he internalizes all his job fears, frustrations, and disappointments.

Thus, he has a unique way of blinding himself to reality, which prevents adaptation to the situation. What appears to be stoic acceptance of his current work situation is not the case at all. He has simply diverted his feelings to a subconscious level; by pushing his feelings further back into his subconscious mind, his pain has manifested itself in the form of functional ailments.

Regression. Another defense mechanism for nonacceptance of reality is reversion to immature behavior. Unable to cope with nonpromotability, some individuals return to reaction patterns that gave them comfort or relief at an earlier period in their lives.

"Because he hasn't gotten promoted, he's been acting like a child." That's how a manager described one subordinate who was showing signs of becoming a lifer—he was regressing in his thinking and actions instead of progressing. The manager explained:

Let me tell you how he's been behaving and you'll see what I mean. After I turned him down for promotion, he stopped talking to me. Oh, he would answer questions when they were directed specifically to him. Otherwise, he had few words to exchange with me. Believing that he would get over that nonsense, I thought it would be helpful to give him a feeling of importance by assigning him the task of breaking in some new people in the department. But instead of helping them, he spent almost all his time with them boasting about his past accomplishments.

Another thing he did that made him the target of private jokes was to become extraordinarily status conscious. He decorated his office by bringing in furnishings from home and hanging every plaque and sign of recognition he had ever earned. And he was fussy about who sat next to him at lunch or who ate lunch with him. He wanted to mix only with the brass. He also expected to be treated royally by suppliers and subordinates.

He was intolerable when anybody disagreed with him. He'd get angry and storm out of your office. On occasion, he would become so emotional that you had the feeling he was going to break out in tears. And if you crossed him in a business argument, he took it personally.

He became a master at evading responsibility. He didn't want any problems or headaches. If a task became too tough, he simply dropped it. If something looked like it might be difficult to do, he balked at doing it.

What really surprised me most was his increasing self-indulgence. He began to overeat, drink too much, and play too hard. He let his hair grow longer, started dressing in a mod way, and began to think of himself as the company Lothario.

The transformation in the man was remarkable. He acted as though he were experiencing a second childhood, one I doubt he was enjoying. I know none of us was enjoying it.

COPING with COMMON REACTIONS

The idea of being nonpromotable leaves most people hurt and stunned. Recovery depends on your ability to recognize reality and cope with it. To the extent that you deny it and try to fight it, the effect can be immobilizing. The patterns discussed are natural defense mechanisms. They become unnatural or abnormal when they are extended beyond a reasonable period of adjustment.

The basis of the common reaction patterns to the realization that one is nonpromotable is a need for some form of escape or a not-so-positive attempt to regain self-esteem or get rid of frustration. Knowing when to back off or hold down these self-defeating reactions can make the difference between becoming a lifer and being a well-adjusted person who copes successfully with the knowledge that one will probably never be promoted.

Avoiding the Escape Route

Struggling to escape a career impasse is understandable. In fact, those who accept it too readily are vulnerable to premature nonpromotability. Escaping temporarily buys you time to make difficult adjustments.

The contrast between healthy and unhealthy forms of escape is dramatized by these two examples.

Unhealthy. After realizing that his career had reached an impasse in his present company, Mike made a series of job changes, each a few years apart. None of them accomplished what he was seeking.

During this period of time, he became very active in industry organizations in an attempt to establish his reputation and make contacts. This opened some doors for him, but it didn't win him a promotion.

In time, he shifted his attention from moving ahead on the job to gaining prominence within the organizations he had joined. Increasingly, he spent less time on job-related activities and more time on outside organization-related activities.

Healthy. Recognizing his nonpromotability, Jim considered quitting his job and starting fresh somewhere else. However, after investigating several possibilities, he realized that he would only succeed in making lateral moves that offered little improvement over his current situation.

After years of struggling to succeed, one of Jim's initial reactions to the realization that he had lost his career momentum was to say, "The hell with it all." His main interest had been work; now he could spend more time with the family, travel, and enjoy life. For awhile, that's exactly what he did. However, after just a few months, he knew that treating his work casually hurt his performance. Even more importantly, by treating it less importantly, work had become less important to him. It didn't maintain his interest; didn't challenge him; it began to bore him. He therefore tried to establish a balance — work was still important to him and so were the things he was now doing off the job. He planned to fill his days with sufficient quantities of both kinds of activities to give himself a sense of satisfaction and fulfillment.

Restoring Your Self-Esteem

The reason acceptance of nonpromotability is so difficult for most of us is that it damages our self-esteem. Somebody is telling you, "You're not good enough to go any higher up the executive ladder. You're a washout." No wonder you're determined to prove otherwise. What you do to reestablish your self-esteem may be either self-defeating or self-enhancing.

Building your current position is a common way of trying to reestablish your self-esteem. Beware when these esteem-seeking activities include excessive politicking and empire building, both of which are self-defeating. The best way to lose friends and influence people unfavorably is to satisfy your own interests at their expense.

The director of a quality-control department discovered how self-defeating politicking and empire building can be. He was in the unique position to give "fits" to other departments, particularly sales and manufacturing. By being overly zealous in performing his job, rejecting products for borderline deficiencies, he could wield power. He also found that by appealing to top management's fear of quality slippage, he was able to build up his budget and add unnecessary staff. His antagonism toward other departments and his patent attempts at empire building provoked confrontations and made him disliked and isolated.

Finding a Way to Release Positive Energy

Restoring your self-esteem by making yourself more important to the company is a positive action that brings positive results.

Ted had been a solid performer and was well regarded by the people who worked with him. Several years ago when he was appointed systems manager of the EDP department, his self-esteem was riding high. But recently, when he learned that he was rated nonpromotable on the departmental work force chart, his self-esteem naturally fell. Although only in his mid-thirties, he felt all he had to look forward to was retirement.

Fortunately, with the help of supportive friends and family, Ted decided to take some self-enhancing action. If he was stuck in the systems department, he was going to be the best systems man in the industry. He devoted his time and attention to accomplishing that goal.

He was working for the benefit of both himself and the company, so how could he lose? As he became more important to the company, he felt better about himself, and everybody thought more of him.

The response to nonpromotability is often a flurry of activity — some self-defeating and some self-enhancing. It's the rare man or woman who feels that nothing has changed and keeps "doing business as usual." It's much more common to feel, "I'm nonpromotable! I'd better do something about it."

This need to do something, to blow off steam and release energy, is translated into many different kinds of off-the-job activities: travel, recreation, involvement in community affairs, learning activities, spending time with family and friends, hobbies, and even taking second jobs or starting a part-time business. In moderation, none of these activities is harmful. However, if "nonwork" crowds out "work," absorbing your energy, interests, and creativity, these activities can turn work into something unpleasant and unbearable.

Certainly, after recognizing that you have become nonpromotable, it makes sense to reassess your values. Perhaps you have been devoting too much attention to work. However, creating a nonwork imbalance can turn you into a lifer. And that's something to worry about!

Nonpromotability is not a tragedy. Nor is it something to be welcomed or accepted prematurely. To cope with the strong feelings it evokes requires both self-control and maturity. It's fearsome only to those who don't learn how to deal with it, and who wear blinders that keep them from recognizing its impact. Pity them, because they become lifers!

CHAPTER TWELVE

Adapting Successfully to Nonpromotability

You've invested years in your company, have accumulated benefits, and feel relatively secure. You like the surroundings, the location, and the people you work with. After considerable hard work, you've reached a level in the company that allows you to support a decent standard of living. Although things haven't turned out exactly the way you want them, they could be much worse.

If you leave your current job, you face the unknown. You risk the advantages you have earned and might disrupt your way of life. In a new job, you'll have to prove yourself to strangers who may expect more than you can give. Thus, regardless of the negatives in your current job, the positives outweigh them, and you're not planning to quit.

Because you are frozen in your job, it's important that you make the most of the situation by learning to adapt successfully. Although you won't be changing jobs, your job will be changing continually. The demands of the job won't remain the same. During the remainder of your career you'll probably work for different bosses who have varying expectations. And the company itself will be adapting to its own rate of growth, to a dynamic marketplace, and to the shifting mix of people that shape its structure, policies, and procedures.

As I explained in the previous chapter, if your career has stalled, there are strong forces that could negatively affect your productivity, job satisfaction, and temperament. You may feel that your job, boss, and the company have soured.

My job used to mean much more to me than it does now. It's become a drag. There are many things about it that have become annoying and irritating.

My current boss can't compare to my past boss. He doesn't understand me, is highly critical, and expects me to perform miracles. My old boss trusted me and gave me more freedom of action. The new boss controls me so tightly he smothers me.

This used to be a great company to work for, but they've grown so rapidly, the personal touch has been lost. What used to be a very friendly atmosphere has been spoiled by ambitious newcomers who are forever politicking.

For many people who spend their careers in the same job, the past becomes "the good old days" — that's when they were regarded as "comers." Now, in their eyes, nothing can compare with the glorified past.

However, it's not your job, boss, or company that have soured. You have! You choose to feel as you do. This is a very important concept. Think about it. You can make yourself happy or unhappy about your work situation, depending on how you choose to react to it.

Whereas you can't change the external aspects of your job, such as your salary, the work itself, constraints, and so forth, you can change how you feel about them. Instead of thinking, "This is the way things are and they won't get better," you can ask yourself, "What can I do to change how I feel? What will help me to adapt better? How can I get more satisfaction from my job?"

The following case histories contrast the feelings of two accountants who work for the same auditing firm and perform comparable jobs. One of the accountants started with the company about ten years ago; the other started a few months after the first. They both advanced from junior accountants to senior accountants. Their current salaries are identical. Neither expects future advancement. Many better qualified men are vying for the few partnership openings.

Ed hates his job. He feels he's a failure because his career has stopped progressing. He has tried to find a better job, but has been unsuccessful. He resents his clients who make much more money than he does and enjoy the luxuries that come with success. He doesn't have a good opinion of himself because he has stayed with the company. Although he tells colleagues, "I should have left this company a long time ago," he doesn't believe a job change would have made much difference in his career. He knows he has average ability and is making as much money as he could in a comparable job elsewhere.

If you talk to his co-worker Sam, it's hard to believe that he works in the same job for the same company. He's enthusiastic and enjoys working with successful clients. He's pleased to be a senior accountant and is proud of his accomplishments.

He realizes that it's unlikely he'll become a partner in his current company, but he doesn't brood about it. He feels he makes a decent living and maintains a good way of life. He doesn't care how much he makes compared to others.

Because he's happy with what he's doing, he's much more pleasant to be with than Ed. He gets along well with everybody, including the senior partners who don't think he's promotable. He feels that even if he isn't qualified to be a partner, he's a valuable member of the firm and a qualified accountant. He's not worried about his future. He concentrates on doing a good job today.

Sam chose to focus on the present, to accept things "as is," and live with them. He chose to be happy and behaved accordingly. He made other people feel good and they responded well to him, reinforcing his own good feelings. On the other hand, by worrying about the past and the future, Ed created his present problems. He chose to make himself unhappy and acted in a self-defeating way.

CHOOSING the RIGHT FEELINGS

Choosing right feelings is essential to adapting successfully to nonpromotability. The questionnaire in Worksheet 12 will help you to test your ability to differentiate right from wrong feelings. Work rapidly in classifying all 20 statements as either "right" or "wrong."

WORKSHEET 12
Choosing right feelings.

	Right	Wrong
I should excel in most work tasks.	___	___
I'm as good as anybody, regardless of their intelligence and abilities.	___	___
I can't help myself from reacting badly when things go wrong.	___	___
I can accept myself "as is."	___	___
I can't take pride in my job because I haven't geen given more responsibility.	___	___
I judge myself by what others think of me.	___	___
My boss should be responsible for my development.	___	___
My boss doesn't think much of me, because he hasn't promoted me.	___	___
My duties are described fully by my job description.	___	___
People in higher jobs are happier than I.	___	___
I don't need increasing external rewards to perform well.	___	___
My job is more rewarding now than in the past.	___	___
My personal goals are compatible with company goals.	___	___
To get along successfully in my company, you must be savvy to game-playing.	___	___
I'm boxed in by company policies and procedures.	___	___
I'm important to the company, regardless of my promotability status.	___	___
The company hasn't been fair to me.	___	___
If I dislike basic things about my boss, I can't work well with him/her.	___	___
My own work standards should be higher than my boss's expectations.	___	___
My job is boring.	___	___

I should excel in most work tasks. Wrong. A common reaction to nonpromotability is an I'll-show-you attitude. But striving for perfection can only lead to disappointment. There're some things you do well, and other things you don't. You'll be much happier if you make reasonable demands on yourself.

I'm as good as anybody, regardless of their intelligence and abilities. Right. Your feelings of self-worth shouldn't be dependent on comparisons with other people. So what if others are smarter and have more and better skills? Your self-worth is determined by you. Unfavorable comparisons with more talented people should not damage your opinion of yourself.

I can't help myself from reacting badly when things go wrong. Wrong. Remember, you are the master of your feelings. You may or may not be able to control external events, but you can control how you feel about them. If you say to yourself, "Things went wrong, but I choose not to get upset about them," you increase your adaptability.

I can accept myself "as is." Right. Denying your imperfections won't make them disappear. By recognizing them, you acknowledge the fact that you're human. Everybody's imperfect. Of course, if the defects cause you continuing discomfort, make an attempt to correct them. However, whether successful or not in making corrections, accept yourself.

I can't take pride in my job because I haven't been given increased responsibility. Wrong. You can take pride in anything you feel you do well that is worth doing. The notion that your job must bet "bigger and better" will make work intolerable. Well-adjusted, mature people can enjoy feelings of pride from modest accomplishments.

I judge myself by what others think of me. Wrong. Even if others were qualified to judge you accurately, which most people aren't, it would be foolish to entrust your self-worth to their judgment. You are the best judge of your personal worth. Make certain you don't undervalue it. A person who thinks well of himself is more likely to live up to his expectations. He will also be careful about damaging his self-worth, or letting others damage it.

My boss should be responsible for my development. Wrong. It's great when your boss takes an active part in helping you to develop, but the responsibility is yours. Without your cooperation, nobody can develop you. Yet, you don't need anybody's help for self-development.

My boss doesn't think much of me as he hasn't promoted me. Wrong. Your boss may consider you invaluable in your current job and that you're making a major contribution. However, he may feel you aren't qualified for a higher-level job that requires skills other than those that have served you well in the past. Your relationship with him will become strained if you allow yourself to believe he doesn't think much of you because he hasn't promoted you.

My duties are described fully by my job description. Wrong. A job description is, at best, a rough guideline to the scope of your responsibilities. Within any job description, there is considerable opportunity for broadening your job. By interpreting a job description narrowly, you restrict yourself unnecessarily. With imagination, even the dullest job description can be enriched.

People in higher jobs are happier than I. Wrong. Promotion can be the surest route to unhappiness. The new job may require sacrifices you are not prepared to make—longer hours, time away from the family, heavy travel, and so forth. It also may tax your capabilities and shake your confidence in yourself. The Peter Principle has been proved time and time again. People often rise to their level of incompetence. By not advancing, you may be saving yourself a lot of headaches. Unfortunately, the nonpromotable who covets higher jobs he can't handle causes himself grief.

I don't need increasing external rewards to perform well. Right. Motivation comes from within. Whereas external rewards, such as money, recognition, and status, can help coax that motivation from you, you can be well motivated without the need for external rewards. Self-fulfillment and personal satisfaction can be powerful motivators.

My job is more rewarding now than in the past. Right. The expression, "It's not getting older, it's getting better" is the right way to feel about your job. Don't be like the man who married a ravishing beauty and became disenchanted as she aged. You should shift your emphasis to aspects of your job that strengthen with age.

My personal goals are compatible with company goals.
Right. By aligning your personal goals with the company
goals, you can work for both of them simultaneously. When
personal and company goals conflict, you're pulled in opposite
directions. Don't let a gap occur between them.

*To get along successfully in my company, you must be
savvy to game-playing.* Right. Being functional is important to
the adaptable promotable. One of the advantages of being in
an organization for a long time, particularly in the same job, is
that you learn how to avoid mixing in politics. But it's wise to
know who's campaigning as well as the major issues.

I'm boxed in by company policies and procedures. Wrong.
Company policies and procedures can be interpreted freely
and can be stretched with impunity. The nonpromotable who
feels boxed in will behave accordingly, making the company
environment stultifying. In contrast, the nonpromotable who
learns how to stretch the rules legitimately gives himself
greater freedom of action.

*I'm important to the company, regardless of my promot-
ability status.* Right. You're as important as the contributions
you make. As long as you develop your skills and apply them
wisely, you'll be an important asset. The company needs its
chiefs, but it also needs its subchiefs and its indians.

The company hasn't been fair to me. Wrong. One expression that can destroy your peace of mind is, "That's not fair!"
Inequities are impossible to avoid. Even in the smallest company, the complex network of personal relationships leads to
numerous examples of "unfair" corporate justice. Righeous in-
dignation rarely does much good, and it makes you unhappy.
The adaptable nonpromotable has the resilience and maturity
to live with inequities. Naturally, if there is a reasonable
chance of appealing or overturning an unfair action, by all
means fight for justice. But jousting with windmills accomplishes nothing except an increase in your dissatisfaction.

*If I dislike basic things about my boss, I can't work well
with him.* Wrong. Even people you love, such as your family
and close friends, possess characteristics you dislike. But, you
overlook those flaws because you value the relationship. Instead of focusing on what you dislike about your boss, try to

find things about him that you can like. It will make it much easier to work with him.

My own work standards should be higher than my boss's expectations. Right. A popular misconception is that most supervisors insist on high standards. Generally, your boss will be satisfied with a mediocre performance, particularly as performance measurement can be highly subjective. If the boss likes you, you can get by with a minimally acceptable effort. But the problem with coasting, doing less than you're capable of, is that you lose competence. By setting your own high standards, you protect your competence and enjoy the satisfaction of achievement.

My job is boring. Wrong. Regardless of how routine your job is, it's not boring. Whenever feelings of boredom creep up on you, challenge yourself: "Why do I choose to be bored by my work? How can I do routine tasks in new and different ways?" Otherwise, your feelings of boredom can turn your job into drudgery, and you'll suffer through every work day.

For each statement of feelings you identified correctly as right or wrong, score five points. If you scored 90 points or better, the probability that you will adapt well or are adapting well to remaining in the same position is excellent. If you scored less than 90 points, but higher than 70 points, you may have some problems adapting and should try to change those feelings that create problems for you. If you scored less than 70 points, your feelings will work against your successful adaptation to nonpromotability. To avoid future job dissatisfaction, pay close attention to the remainder of this chapter. It can help you develop an action plan to cope with self-defeating feelings.

THE JOB INVENTORY

Everybody should periodically take inventory of his job. The purpose of this procedure is to make sure that you have plentiful sources of satisfaction in your daily work life. Sit down with a pad of paper and sharp pencils in a quiet place where you won't be interrupted. Tear off the first sheet of paper, fold it lengthwise, and at the top label it Kicks. In the left-hand column, list those things you do daily that are a

source of enjoyment. In the right-hand column, describe why
a particular activity makes you feel good. A typical Kicks List
might look like this:

PEOPLE CONTACT   I enjoy making friends. I like
                                  to belong to a group. I feel im-
                                  portant when I'm helping
                                  others. It's nice to have friends
                                  to help me when I'm having
                                  problems.

CREATIVE WORK   I like to use my imagination.
                                  It's exciting to come up with a
                                  new twist in an old way of
                                  doing something.

INDEPENDENCE   I like to feel that my boss
                                  trusts me and has confidence in
                                  me. I want to be able to iden-
                                  tify accomplishments for which
                                  I am solely responsible.

CHALLENGE   I like change and variety in my
                                  job. I like to learn new things
                                  and to apply new knowledge.

Take a second sheet of paper, fold it lengthwise, and at the
top label it Bug List. On the left-hand side, list all the things in
your daily work life that annoy and worry you. In the right-
hand column, explain why. Completing the right-hand side,
the list would look like this:

MENIAL WORK   The prospect of doing the same
                                  thing day in and day out really
                                  bugs me. I feel I'm wasting my
                                  talents. I'm capable of doing
                                  more important projects.

CLOSE SUPERVISION   When my boss watches me too
                                  closely, I feel insecure. Be-
                                  cause I don't want to make a
                                  mistake, I try to second-guess
                                  him and do what I think he
                                  wants. This makes me feel
                                  guilty because I feel I'm not
                                  my own person.

ENDLESS PROJECTS	I don't like projects that never seem to end, stretching from day to day. I feel I'm not accomplishing anything.
POWER AND AUTHORITY	I don't like to feel like a mindless robot. It bugs me when my boss gives me an order and doesn't explain why I should carry it out.

Take a third piece of paper, fold it lengthwise, and label it Show-Off List. Identify the activities that give you a sense of pride. These are things that you know you do well and in which you like to show off your skills. Explain why you feel these are your strengths. A Show-Off List might include:

TALKING	I express myself well. In college I was on the debating team and was active in dramatics. In formal or informal presentations, my past training is apparent.
NEGOTIATING	Everybody says I have the gift of the blarney. In striking a bargain my powers of persuasion really shine.
SOCIAL EASE	I relate well to people. I'm a good conversationalist and I'm well liked. I feel at ease in groups and am usually the center of attraction.
COMPETITIVENESS	I respond well to competition; I display extraordinary energy and endurance. Everybody around here calls me a "money player." If there's a contest, I'll be in the winner's circle.

On a fourth piece of paper, compile your last list, the Under-the-Carpet List, on which you describe qualities you'd like to hide. Follow the same procedures as with the previous lists. For example:

WORKING WITH NUMBERS	I'm slow at working with numbers and am notoriously inaccurate.
HANDLING DETAILS	I'm good at initiating projects, but I tend to be careless with follow-through details.
ORDERLINESS	I'm disorganized and tend to act without formal planning.
ADAPTABILITY	Once I make up my mind, I'm not easy to change. Some of my co-workers have accused me of being stubborn.

Armed with these four lists, you can prepare a daily work balance sheet like the one shown in Worksheet 13. On the left side of the balance sheet, record daily activities which appear on either your Kicks List or your Show-Off List. Indicate how much time you spent at these activities. For example, you attended a meeting in which you had an opportunity for people contact and to show off your verbal and social skills. You also had an opportunity to visit a key customer and use your skills as a negotiator. You spent a total of 270 minutes on activities that you like and do well.

On the right-hand side, list daily activities that are on your Bug List or your Under-the-Carpet List, or both. For example, you had to prepare a customer proposal that required you to fuss with details and numbers. This activity took 180 minutes.

On balance, this was a good day. You spent 270 minutes doing things you consider to be positive, and only 180 minutes doing things you consider to be negative.

Maintaining a daily work balance sheet helps you to get a better perspective on your job. It helps you to spot developing imbalances quickly. Naturally, imbalances on the right side are your major concern. When you spend too much time doing things that you don't like and don't do well, your job is less satisfying. To correct the imbalance, plan counterbalancing activities for the left side (that is, kicks and show-off activities).

Once you get the swing of this simple system, you'll be surprised at how much you can control your work day. Instead of griping about "how bad things are," you can take positive action to make things better.

WORKSHEET 13
Daily work balance sheet.

Kicks and show-off activities		Bug list and under-the-carpet activities	
ACTIVITY	DURATION	ACTIVITY	DURATION
Attended meeting	90 min	Prepared customer proposal	180 min
Visited key customer	180 min		
Total minutes	270	Total minutes	180

RETHINKING VALUES

The great American work values, "get ahead" and "get rich," drive us mercilessly. How far ahead? How rich? Who determines the standards for these values? For most people, somebody else is calling the signals. In the media, you read about and see the benefits of becoming successful. At work, there are many models for you to emulate — rapidly rising executives winning prestige, power, and financial rewards.

You're influenced by the aspirations of ambitious peers. Your friends glorify advancement. You're being pulled and pushed ahead, sacrificing personal time, your peace of mind, and, sometimes, family relationships and your self-respect.

To adapt successfully to your future, now is the time to become a self-determiner. Why? Because you have no choice. You have reached your career limits. Your future depends on your adaptability. Unadaptable people become lifers waiting for their careers to end. Others quit their jobs and throw themselves into unemployment. Adaptable people learn to do what Nena and George O'Neill call centering.° This is the process of deciding what you really feel, want, and need. You need to rethink your basic values and find new ones that will serve you better in the future.

What new values are relevant to you? Discard old values dictated by other people. Forget about what they think are important. You have to discover what's right for yourself.

Start on the way to self-discovery with this simple exercise. First ask yourself how you feel about being nonpromotable and record your answers in writing:

I feel frustrated.
I feel angry.
I feel unhappy.
I feel I'm a failure.
I feel forgotten.
I feel unimportant.
I feel insecure.
I feel concerned about the future.

Unless you're unique, most of your feelings about being nonpromotable are negative. It's disturbing to know you will not be promoted beyond your current position; thinking about it evokes strong emotions. None of these negative feelings will do you any good. They block successful adaptation to the situation. Try to substitute positive feelings for them:

°Nena O'Neill and George O'Neill, *Shifting Gears* (New York: M. Evans, 1974), 255 pp.

I feel it's great to stop worrying about getting ahead.
I feel content with what I've got.
I feel I'm successful.
I feel important.
I feel I'm growing personally and will continue to grow in the future.
I feel my job can be as stimulating and challenging as I want to make it.

The second step in the self-discovery exercise is to make a list of the things you believe you want from your job:

I want to make enough money to support a good life-style.
I want to get along well with my boss and my co-workers.
I want job security.
I want to take pride in my work.
I want variety in my work.
I want freedom of action.
I want to be able to make decisions independently.
I want recognition.
I want respect.
I want to do meaningful work.

Now comes the most important step in the exercise. Define your personal wants specifically. What are the lowest acceptable limits of each of these wants? Are your lowest acceptable limits reasonably attainable? Which of your personal wants must you have in order to be satisfied with your job? Which are desirable, but can be lived without? What kind of job performance will earn you most of your personal wants? How will improving your performance and increasing your job skills help you to earn more of your personal wants? Can you foresee circumstances that may require you to change your personal wants?

The following case histories illustrate how important it is to define your personal wants.

Ralph and Mitch are nonpromotables. Their personal wants are similar. However, their situations are quite different. Both men had listed among their wants that they wanted their jobs to support their current life-styles. At the time that Ralph made that statement he was living in an exclusive neighborhood in a house he could barely afford. He had a large mortgage and heavy real estate taxes. Furthermore, he had outstanding loans on a new car and home furnishings. He was a member of a country club and enjoyed a heavy entertainment schedule.

As the cost of living skyrocketed and two of his four children entered college, he found it increasingly difficult to manage his finances. The contrast between his own tight financial budget and that of his prosperous neighbors was upsetting to him. Recently, he confronted his boss; he explained his financial problems and asked for a salary increase. He was told that he was already at the upper limits of his salary range.

Although Mitch's income is comparable to Ralph's, supporting his lifestyle has been much easier. He has lived in the same modest house for nearly 20 years. The mortgage is low and almost paid. And although his real estate taxes have gone up, they are still considerably lower than Ralph's. Mitch has no outstanding loans because he prefers to save for big purchases. He lives in a neighborhood in which most of the people enjoy a decent standard of living but are content to live modestly.

Mitch has three children in college. Years ago, he invested in mutual funds to guarantee enough money for their freshman and sophomore years. Thereafter, he felt that his children would manage to complete their education by working part time and, if necessary, taking student loans. Although his salary hasn't progressed much, Mitch continues to get along well on his income; he manages all his expenses and saves about 5 percent of net income each year.

On their respective want lists, both men indicated that they wanted to get along well with their boss and co-workers. Ralph is having difficulty satisfying this want; Mitch is happy with his own work situation.

In Ralph's department, there has been heavy turnover. He complains that he hardly knows the people in the department. His friends have either moved up or out of the company. In the last five years he's had two bosses. He used to enjoy the feeling of belonging to a cohesive work group and working for mature, understanding bosses. He doesn't like the newcomers as well and, by his own admission, hasn't tried to make friends with them. As a result, work is not as much fun as it used to be.

Mitch has also watched people come and go in his department. And he, too, has worked under several bosses. But he welcomes the change of people. It gives him a chance to expand his circle of friends and meet new and interesting people. Because most of the newcomers are younger than he, he has become a respected senior member of the group. He readily shares his experiences with them, and they welcome his advice.

Another want that both men shared was job security. Ralph has become increasingly insecure, whereas Mitch feels that his own position is "more solid than ever."

Ralph hasn't tried to keep up to date. He rarely reads or spends any time in self-development. The few times the company has given him any special training, he resented the time away from home and didn't try to apply any new methods back on the job. Although he's unaware of the fact that he's been losing his level of competence, he does know that his performance is slipping. In fact, he has been warned about that fact by his boss on several occasions. He's worried about it, but he's not sure of what to do. He feels the boss doesn't like him personally.

In contrast, Mitch has been determined to protect his competence. He feels that as long as he performs well, his job is safe. He reads regularly and has taken courses at a local university. In addition, whenever the company offers a special training course he jumps at the opportunity. And on returning to the job, he increases his effectiveness by putting his new knowledge to work. His performance is consistently good, and his annual appraisals attest to that fact.

In preparing want lists, both Mitch and Ralph said that they wanted challenging and stimulating jobs and a sense of accomplishment. A few years later, Ralph feels shortchanged, whereas Mitch has realized his wants.

Seeing his job as a dead end, Ralph feels, "There's no sense in breaking my back." He does what he's told—and no more. He evades new responsibilities and "too much work pressure." He's a master buckpasser and manages to dump assignments on other people. Of course he's bored and doesn't have a feeling of accomplishment because he has made it clear that he doesn't want to be bothered with "anything out of the ordinary."

Unlike Ralph, Mitch welcomes new projects. He rushes through his routine tasks so that he'll be available to assume new responsibilities. Because of his capacity for work, his boss tends to load him up with assignments. To keep on top of the work load, he works hard during the day and sometimes has to work overtime or bring work home. But that's okay with him. He likes to be busy and involved with his job. When coworkers needle him about being a work horse, he has a stock answer that reflects his attitude: "I work for a demanding boss —myself!"

The last item that appeared on the want list of both men was the statement, "I want freedom of action and independence." Ralph has been losing his freedom of action and independence, whereas Mitch has made substantial gains.

Over the years, Ralph has become careless in his work habits. The thoroughness of his work and its accuracy have slipped. He turns in work assignments at the very last minute or behind schedule. These performance deficiencies prompted his previous bosses to supervise him closely. This set up a vicious cycle: Since he was being watched closely, he felt there was no need to check his own work. As he said, "It's going to be checked anyway." So he gives assignments a "once-over-lightly." He's not interested in doing more than an acceptable job. Thus, his work prompts closer supervision.

Mitch's work habits are very different. He's very thorough, meticulous, and reliable. He double-checks everything and, because of his long experience in the same job, requires minimal instruction. When he's uncertain about something, he'll ask questions. Otherwise, he'll work things out by himself.

Because of Mitch's reliability, his boss manages him with a very light touch. He gives him greater freedom of action and independence than anybody else in the department. By earning his boss's confidence and respect, he has won special treatment.

INTERNAL CONTROL
RATHER THAN EXTERNAL CONTROL

Nonpromotability is difficult to accept. Only by learning to adapt to it can you hope to cope with it successfully. You have little control over the "givens" in a work environment. You can't avoid basic work requirements. You can't do much, if anything, to influence compensation, your boss's work style, company policies and procedures, and the other externals. But you can exert the most important kind of control—internal control.

Whatever external environment you face, you can choose how you want to react to it. You can select feelings that enable you to maintain a high level of personal satisfaction. And you can adopt new values and modified personal wants that will help you to adapt.

Adaptation, by definition, is "adjusting oneself to different conditions, environment, etc." By gaining better control of yourself, instead of struggling futilely against the work environment, you can master nonpromotability.

CHAPTER THIRTEEN

Life and Career Planning

When your career growth stops, you may believe that it's a waste of time to make any future career plans. At this point you feel you should know what to expect in the future from your job, boss, and company.

Maybe things will go as you expect, but they probably won't. By completing the questionnaire in Worksheet 14, you'll appreciate how many important changes you may have to contend with in the future.

Even if you stay in your current job until you retire, the chances that you'll outgrow the job or the job will outgrow you are high. As your company reacts to business cycles and technological changes, it will have to hire and fire people and restructure jobs and working relationships. The only thing that is certain about the future is change.

Life and career planning is the way you can anticipate, prepare for, and influence change. By thinking out beforehand what actions you'll take under varying contingencies, you gain precious time to analyze potential problems, consider alternatives, and gather facts to help strengthen your decisions.

WHY WE AVOID
LIFE and CAREER PLANNING

You may have doubts about the benefits of formal life and career planning. Probably you're more accustomed to informal

WORKSHEET 14
Calculating the probabilities of career change.

What are the probabilities:

1. You'll stay in your current job until you retire?

   ☐ High   ☐ Medium   ☐ Low

2. You'll outgrow your job?

   ☐ High   ☐ Medium   ☐ Low

3. Your job will outgrow you?

   ☐ High   ☐ Medium   ☐ Low

4. Your company will change its policies and procedures, affecting you in some way?

   ☐ High   ☐ Medium   ☐ Low

5. You'll always work under the same boss?

   ☐ High   ☐ Medium   ☐ Low

6. Your feelings about your job and/or company will change?

   ☐ High   ☐ Medium   ☐ Low

7. Your company will reorganize, affecting your job status?

   ☐ High   ☐ Medium   ☐ Low

8. You will continue to work with the same people indefinitely?

   ☐ High   ☐ Medium   ☐ Low

9. Your job will stay exactly the same?

   ☐ High   ☐ Medium   ☐ Low

10. Economic booms and depressions and technological changes will affect the company and you?

   ☐ High   ☐ Medium   ☐ Low

planning. For example, you would like to send your children to college at some time in the future. So you save a few dollars each paycheck. That's life planning. You've anticipated a need and are preparing to meet it.

Similarly, you may currently be using skills on your job that are becoming obsolete. Realizing that you'll have to acquire new skills, you enroll in a part-time program at a local university. That's career planning. Once again, you've recognized a developing need and have acted now in preparation for the future.

Much of the informal planning you do naturally involves clearly defined needs that you respond to automatically, without considering alternatives. Sometimes it works well. But when the problems facing you aren't easily identified and defined, and you're uncertain as to the best action to take, you can no longer rely on your natural planning instincts.

Yet, you may be reluctant to try formal life and career planning. You may share the feeling of a young woman who confided in me during a counseling interview, "I can appreciate the need to plan specific work-related problems, but I have a hang-up about life and career planning. I feel my future is so uncertain, I can't make predictions with any degree of accuracy. I'm not even certain about what's going to happen next week. How can I possibly know what's going to happen in three years, five years, or ten years?"

I told her she didn't have to predict the future. It wasn't necessary to do so. As we discussed it, she saw that all she had to do was make reasonable assumptions based on the futurity of events that have already occurred. She realized that she could apply this line of reasoning to her own situation:

Let's see if I understand you. I supervise the sales analysis department. We abstract data from computer reports and rework and interpret them. From discussions I've had with the director of sales administration, he feels much of what we do can be done faster and more accurately by the computer. It might take years, but it's highly probable that the computer will replace us. Using that as a reasonable working assumption, I have to start thinking now about what I'll do when that happens.

Another reason you may avoid formal planning is that you find the prospect of change frightening:

There are too many changes around here! Management makes sweeping changes and expects me to take them in stride. I don't want to relearn how to get my job done. I trust routines I know well.

You resist change because it introduces the elements of uncertainty and risk. It forces you to abandon old, familiar ways and arouses unpleasant emotions. For example, a nonpromotable who had worked under the same man for nearly ten years described his feelings when he got a new boss:

When my boss was promoted, I panicked. He wasn't perfect, but I knew how to work with him. There were no surprises. I knew his moods and could predict his actions. I didn't know what to expect from a new boss. I was concerned about having to gain his trust and confidence and having to prove myself all over again.

Change is particularly threatening when it forces you to acquire new skills. One day you're confident of your competence; then suddenly you're a fumbling duffer with two left hands. For example, the advertising manager in a medium-size packaged goods company had worked closely for years with a very competent advertising agency. Shortly after a new vice president of marketing was appointed, who had decided that the company could save money by creating an in-house advertising agency, he directed the advertising manager to stop using the agency and recruit people for an in-house program instead. It took almost a year before he felt confident with the new operation.

Sometimes you resist change because it carries with it implied criticism; or it means that your job will become harder to perform; or it disrupts valued interpersonal relationships.

IMPLIED CRITICISM
"Nobody explained why my duties were being changed. I was concerned that it meant I wasn't doing a good job."

HARDER JOB
"The change in the reporting procedure will double my work load."

DISRUPTED INTERPERSONAL RELATIONSHIPS
"I really enjoyed working with the people in the order processing department. When I switched to the distribution department, I felt cut off from my friends."

A common reason for choosing to avoid formal life and career planning is simply that you have developed bad habits. You're used to making quick decisions, either without consciously planning them or after very little thought. Generally, you consider a limited number of alternatives and often just a single alternative, especially in reaction to a crisis. In a frantic effort to deal with the crisis, you tend to oversimplify the situation by searching for easy-to-solve problems.

THE PLANNING PAYOFF

Because of the reasons discussed, you may be wary of investing time and effort in life and career planning. Perhaps a review of the payoff for planning will convince you how it can help you.

Improvement in Quality of Life at Work and at Home

By enhancing your ability to choose the right action at the right time, you can improve the quality of your life both at home and at work. Planning forces you to think more seriously about your problems and opportunities; it helps you to consider them in a logical, systematic way, delaying acting until you understand possible actions open to you as well as the probable consequences of each.

More Effective Integration of On-the-Job and Off-the-Job Activities

What you do on the job may conflict with what you want from your life; what you do at home may conflict with what you want from the job. Planning helps you to better integrate work and life activities to achieve a satisfying balance. For example, you may be bored with your job and want an increase in responsibilities. However, a substantial increase in responsibilities could overload you, and force you to give up your free time. Planning will help you decide how much extra responsibility to assume and will improve your job satisfaction without making major sacrifices in your home life.

Better Problem Solving and Decision Making

Planning forces you to select specific, meaningful, and realistic objectives. It helps you to identify problems, define them precisely, and set priorities. It requires that you gather relevant facts from reliable sources. It demands that you develop multiple alternatives, all of which can contribute substantially to the resolution of your problems, and that you select the one that best meets your objectives, fits your resources, and maximizes your decisions.

Greater Personal Flexibility

As part of the planning process, you consider multiple alternatives. Thus, if your plans don't work as expected, you have contingency plans on the shelf. You can make timely changes.

Minimized Risks

The more time you spend thinking about potential problems, the fewer surprises the future is likely to hold. You won't be able to avoid unforeseen events, but you can certainly minimize risks. Suppose your industry's growth rate has been plateauing. By examining the performance of your company relative to other companies in the industry, you can make assumptions about their respective future performances and the impact of a growth rate change on your department and you.

LIFE and CAREER TARGET PLANNING

Worksheet 15 is designed to help you focus your attention on major target areas for your life and career planning. Each of the ten questions on the worksheet deserves your full attention. Work independently, thinking about each question for at least a half hour. After you have completed the worksheet, you might want to share your answers with your immediate family, close friends, or with others you feel are genuinely interested in you and can provide you with better perspective and insights.

Here are some of the factors you should consider:

1. *What major obligations do you feel you may have to meet in the next three to five years?* Will you have to finance a college education for your children? Will you have to assume support for a parent? Will your home require major repairs?

WORKSHEET 15
Life and career planning.

1. What major obligations do you feel you may have to meet in the next three to five years? _____

2. What basic changes in your life-style would you like to make in the next three to five years? _____

3. Will your current rate of financial growth allow you meet your major obligations? _____

4. How will changes in your basic life-style affect your job?

5. In what ways would you like to change your relationship with your boss? _____

6. How would you like to change your relationship with other members of your company? _____

7. What new experiences and/or added responsibilities would you like from your job? _____

8. Would you like to change the tempo of your job in any way?

9. How can you increase your job security? _____

10. How will changes in your job affect your life? _____

Will you have to finance a wedding reception? How will the rising cost of living affect you?

2. *What basic changes in your life-style would you like to make in the next three to five years?* Do you want to buy a bigger house? Do you feel the need to increase the size of your savings? Would you like to take advantage of foreign travel? Would you like to relocate to an area with more desirable climate? Would you like more free time? Would you like to become more involved in community activities?

3. *Will your current rate of financial growth allow you to meet your major obligations?* How much of a salary increase can you expect each year? Are you nearing the maximum of your salary range? Is there an opportunity to earn any extra compensation? Can you supplement your salary with outside income?

4. *How will changes in your basic life-style affect your job?* Will the time demands of off-the-job activities interfere with your job? Will your company allow you to transfer to a more favorable climate? Does the company's vacation policy provide enough time for extended vacations? Do company policies restrict the kinds of outside activities in which you can participate?

5. *In what ways would you like to change your relationship with your boss?* Would you like him to give you greater freedom of action? Would you want him to show greater appreciation for your efforts? Would you like him to be more cooperative with you? Would you like to change his image of you? Do you want to continue to work with him?

6. *In what ways would you like to change your relationship with other members of your company?* Whom would you like to work with more closely? Whose support would you like to gain? Would you like to improve your relationship with members of the company who have been adversaries in the past?

7. *What new experiences and/or added responsibilities would you like from your job?* Would you like to be given special open-ended assignments? Would you like to participate in special project teams? Would you like to perform some of the duties that your boss or other people are currently doing?

8. *Would you want to change the tempo of your job in any way?* Is it too fast or too slow? Would you prefer a more even flow of work? Would you like the tempo to slow down or speed up at certain times of the day or at certain times of the year?

9. *How can you increase your job security?* Would you like to become an authority in one area? Would you like an opportunity to keep up with new developments? Would you like to work in a more stable department?

10. *How will changes in your job affect your life?* To improve relationships with your boss or other members of the company, will you have to socialize with them off the job? Will the demands of your job detract from the time you spend with your family? Will worrying about your job affect how you act at home?

MAKING LIFE and CAREER PLANS

Assuming you're convinced that planning merits an investment of your time and effort, let's consider how to make sound life and career plans. The first step is to make a commitment to spend at least an hour a week, every week, developing and reviewing your plans. Planning should be a continuous process. The plan itself is just a formal record of your planning at a particular point in time. Initially, I recommend that you prepare formal written plans semiannually. Once you have determined your individual planning needs, you may decide on a more or less frequent basis.

Note that I use the words formal and written to describe your plan. It's formal inasmuch as it should adhere to a specific format — objectives, problems, facts, feelings, alternatives, decisions, actions, potential problems, and controls.

The plan must be written because life and career planning is too complicated to do in your head. When you put something down on paper, you can see it, study it, and come back to it as many times as you wish. Furthermore, if you decide to share your projections with other people, it's easier to do so when your plans are written.

Start your plan by considering objectives. What do you want to accomplish? If you have been thorough in completing the life- and career-planning worksheet, you have already identified target areas: meeting major obligations, achieving basic changes in your life-style, improving relations with your boss and other members of your company, gaining new experiences and added responsibilities, changing the tempo of your job, and increasing your job security. With little effort, you can probably compile an extensive list of objectives, but you obviously can't work on all these objectives simultaneously.

In sorting out the four or five initial objectives to be included in your plan, review your full list of objectives and ask yourself, "Which of my objectives will bring a meaningful improvement in the quality of my life or job situation? Are my objectives specific? Realistic? Measurable?" A student in one of my classes who worked for the marketing department of a major chemicals company listed two life objectives and two work objectives, on his first try.

Life objectives
1. I want to send my son to college.
2. I want to spend more time with my family.

Work objectives
1. I want to get more responsibility at work.
2. I want to improve my work relations with the accounting department.

After several discussions, we agreed that the achievement of these objectives would bring about meaningful improvements in his life and work situations. But these objectives were neither specific nor measurable, so he rewrote them:

Life objectives
1. By 1980, I will save $2,000 for my son's first year's tuition at college.
2. During this year, I will spend an average of 10 hours per week with my family in joint activities.

Work objectives
1. By the end of this year, I will identify which of my boss's duties I could do well and would like to do, and convince him to assign at least one new responsibility to me.
2. By the end of this planning period, I will participate in

a minimum of three cooperative projects with the accounting department.

After the objectives have been identified, the next step in developing a plan is to anticipate problems that must be solved in order to accomplish your goals. As problems often come in clusters, you have to be able to sort out the most urgent and serious. It may be possible to work on several problems at one time, but you should usually attack them in sequence. It is therefore important to set priorities; problems should be in order of importance.

When the target problems are identified, describe each in full detail in terms of what's happening? Where? When? For how long? Who's involved? Then consider your chances for success. If you charge head-on into a problem you can't handle, you won't accomplish anything. Save your strength and energy for problems you can solve.

Continuing with the previous example, the following problems are associated with the stated life and career objectives.

Life Objectives

$2,000 in savings for college tuition: The man makes $20,000 a year and expects annual salary increases of $1,000. The problems he faces in accumulating $2,000 in the next three years are: he's currently not saving any money, nor has he been able to save in the last three years; the cost of living is going up at a rate that will more than equal his annual salary increases; and he anticipates some unusually heavy expenses within the next few years (replacing his automobile and repainting his house). As he obviously can't do anything about the rising cost of living, he has decided to concentrate on saving 3 percent of his gross income per year, while meeting his existing expenses and anticipated extraordinary expenses.

Note that he doesn't try to shift his financial problems from himself to his company, by demanding a larger salary. He realizes that he would have virtually no chance of getting an increase in salary and a high probability of hurting his relations with his boss.

Ten hours per week in joint family activities: Both his current life-style and work situation create problems in achieving this objective. Off the job, he spends considerable time on activities that don't involve the family, such as bowling, golf, and involvement in community affairs. On the job, he tends to work long hours and bring work home evenings and weekends. He also has to spend a considerable amount of time in business travel. As long as he stays in his current job, he can't do anything about the travel commitment, so he won't attack that problem. Instead, he'll focus on the problem of trying to reallocate time from his personal activities or work activities, or both, that extend beyond his normal work day. Once again, it is apparent that decisions you make to achieve life objectives may require changes in your job situation.

Work Objectives

New responsibility: Several problems stand in the way of achieving this objective. He doesn't know all the things that his boss does. And he's not certain as to what specific things his boss does that he could do as well or better and would like to do. He also has the problem of finding time to take on new responsibilities; most importantly, he doesn't know under what circumstances his boss would agree to relinquish any responsibility. All these problems will have to be solved, but in a logical sequence. Problem 1 will be to learn more about his boss's job; problem 2, to arrange opportunities to test his own competence and preferences in areas in which his boss functions; problem 3, to examine his present work load to find time for new responsibilities; and problem 4, to convince his boss to relinquish some responsibility.

Cooperative projects with the accounting department: The major problem he faces is a series of past confrontations with members of the accounting department. On most issues, they act as adversaries. Unfortunately, he can't erase the past. However, he wants to improve relations in the future. His first problem is therefore to identify who among the members of the accounting department would most likely be receptive to his attempts at cooperation and to arrange for a fair hearing. Finally, what kinds of joint projects would demonstrate to the other members of the department that he's making an effort to be more cooperative?

Once your objectives are clear, and problems associated

with the objectives are identified and defined precisely,
you're ready to search for facts you need to solve the problems
that stand in your way. Before you go fact-hunting, ask yourself: What questions must be answered? Where can you find
answers? How long will it take to gather the facts? Although
it's desirable to have all relevant data, it may be expedient to
make a decision with some questions unanswered.

When gathering facts, be careful how you process them.
Here are some worthwhile rules to adopt:

> *Challenge the source.* Do you have complete confidence in
> the reliability of the source?
>
> *Always differentiate facts from assumptions.* Too often, as-
> sumptions masquerade as facts.
>
> *Search for bias.* Too many so-called facts are highly subjec-
> tive points of view.
>
> *Don't jump to conclusions.* The facts that get you into trou-
> ble are those that are plausable but not proved.

Let's illustrate these points by continuing a discussion of
the previous example. This individual is faced with the problem of identifying someone in the accounting department who
might be more willing to cooperate with him than are the
other members of the department. Some of the questions that
must be answered to solve this problem are: Who are my most
ardent adversaries in the department? Why are they adversaries? How long have they been opponents? Have they influenced anyone else in the department?

In gathering facts, he reviews past correspondence and minutes of past meetings. He also tries to recall his own past observations and conversations. He discusses his problem with
knowledgeable third parties who offer opinions. In these discussions he searches for the biases of the people who furnish
opinions and labels the information he receives as assumptive
conclusions. For example, "I discussed my problem with Hal
in the EDP department; he believes that my past battles with
Mike in the accounting department have also affected Mary
and Lou. Hal claims that they're all close friends and are
influenced by each other."

After a reasonable amount of time you should have sufficient facts to start considering alternatives. A decision is no better than the alternatives you have evaluated. Preferably, you should explore multiple alternatives, all of which contribute substantially to the resolution of your problem. Then attack them, challenging them strongly. Those alternatives that survive your challenge are most likely to yield satisfactory solutions. The alternative you finally select should be the one that best meets your objectives.

To pick the right alternative, here are some tested methods to use.

List pros and cons. Take a blank sheet of paper and divide it in half. On the left side, list all the reasons for selecting an alternative. On the right side, list all the reasons you shouldn't. If your first impression of the alternative is either pro or con, try to achieve a fair balance by seriously considering the opposite point of view.

Put alternatives aside. It often helps to put alternatives aside for a few days. Then when you reconsider them, your second look may give you quite a different perspective.

Challenge by jury. Sometimes the best way to get new insights into the potential value of alternatives is to ask trusted peers for constructive criticism. You might try this approach: "Here's what I plan to do. Tell me how it might go wrong. Would I be better off if I tried one of the other alternatives?"

Stage a dress rehearsal. This is a variation of challenge by jury. The difference is that the peers you ask for advice are those who will be responsible for implementing the alternative selected. In effect, you're setting up a dress rehearsal, which gives them a chance to preview a proposed action. For example, you gather your family together and tell them that you want to spend more time with them. You then review alternatives with them and ask which ones they feel are most feasible.

Assigning weights and probabilities. When considering multiple alternatives, it's sometimes helpful to assign relative desirability weights as probabilities for success. By multiplying the desirability weights by the assigned probabilities, you can compare the expected values of each alternative mathematically. For example, suppose your objective is to assume new responsibilities, and one of your major problems is getting your boss's agreement. You identify four alternatives:

1. You could try to convince your boss that he will benefit from assigning you new responsibilities. It will release him to do more important things himself. You should be able to give more time and attention to responsibilities that he normally has to do in a rush.

This is a desirable alternative, so you assign it a probability of .75. However, you feel you have only a 50:50 chance of convincing him. Therefore, the expected value of this alternative would be .75 × .50, or .375.

2. You might recruit a third party to help you make a joint presentation to your boss. To your mind this is a less desirable alternative because you would prefer to convince your boss yourself. So you assign it a desirability weight of .50. However, if you pick a person who has influence, you feel that this alternative has a better probability of success. So you assign it a probability of .75. The expected value for this alternative is .375.

3. You could plead with your boss for added responsibility. You prefer not to take this approach, so you assign it a desirability weight of .25. However, you feel that the approach has a 50:50 chance of succeeding. This alternative yields an expected value of .125.

4. You could recruit a third party to represent you, perhaps someone in the personnel department. From a personal point of view, this is not as desirable as presenting yourself or making a joint presentation with somebody else. So you assign this a desirability weight of .25. However, you feel this has a high probability of succeeding, provided you pick the right person — someone whom the boss respects and who is capable of making a strong presentation. You assign this alternative a probability of success of .75. The expected value is .188.

The results of these mathematical comparisons are shown in Figure 10. As you can see, alternatives 1 and 2 yield equal expected values. As you assigned a higher desirability weight to alternative 1, that is the one you would pick.

When there are many alternatives available to you and the desirability weights and probabilities of success differ considerably, it's helpful to quantify your judgments.

FIGURE 10
Evaluating alternatives.

Objective: Assume new responsibility.
Problem: Gaining boss's agreement.

ALTERNATIVE	DESIRABILITY	× PROBABILITY OF SUCCESS	= EXPECTED VALUE
Sell benefits yourself	.75	.50	.375
Get third party to help sell benefits	.50	.75	.375
Ask for boss's help	.25	.50	.125
Recruit third party to represent you	.25	.75	.188

PUTTING YOUR PLAN into ACTION

Once you select an alternative, you should plan the actions you'll take to implement the alternative and the timing of these actions. For example, assume your objective is to increase your job responsibilities. After careful fact-finding, you decided that you would like to represent your boss in some of the meetings he's required to attend. In the past you've heard him complain about the fact that he spends too much time at meetings. You feel you would enjoy attending some of these meetings because it would not only give you an opportunity to interface with other departments but would enhance your status.

You've learned details of what meetings he attends regularly from your boss, his secretary, and people in other departments. You know about how much time he has to spend at these meetings and which ones he enjoys and doesn't enjoy. You also have insights as to his role at these meetings and have some idea of where and when you might be able to substitute for him.

The alternative you selected is to approach your boss by yourself; you will try to convince him that you could relieve him of some of the burdens of his responsibilities. However, rather than putting him on the spot and demanding a "yes" or "no" answer, you try to get him to agree to a small first step in the right direction. You suggest that you might attend a meeting with him as an observer, explaining you could, with proper training and guidance, represent him at some meetings.

This first step could lead to a series of progressively more important steps until you have achieved your objectives. It also serves another important purpose — it allows you to try on the new responsibility for size in a risk-free situation. You'll see if you really would like to acquire the new responsibility and if you'll be able to perform it well.

An important part of the planning process is to take tentative action prior to proposed permanent action. When initiating change in your life or in your career, it's wise to be cautious, to take small steps one at a time and evaluate the results of these steps.

At all times you should try to be alert to new problems that might be created by your actions. To solve one problem at the risk of creating several new, perhaps even more serious problems, just doesn't make sense. So you search for the potential chain reaction that can be triggered inadvertently by the step you are planning. For example, after attending one or two meetings with your boss, you may approach him about representing him at a single meeting. To prepare for that meeting you consider potential problems: What would he want to accomplish at these meetings? How do you make certain that you'll accomplish what your boss wants? What positions will he want you to support? How can you avoid misrepresenting him? What do you have to know in order to represent him adequately? If you state his position, what confrontations are you likely to encounter? How would he expect you to deal with these confrontations? How can you keep him well informed about what went on so he won't feel that he missed anything?

Every new experience presents many potential problems. By thinking about them beforehand, planning what you might do and how you would do it, and perhaps rehearsing different approaches, you'll be better able to cope with them.

The planning process doesn't end once you take a proposed action. Thereafter, you should check periodically to see how well things are working out. Compare what is actually happening with what you had expected to happen. For example, you succeeded in assuming the added responsibility of representing your boss at selected interdepartmental meetings. You're pleased with having the added responsibility and it's accomplishing some of the things that you desired — you're interfacing with influential people in the company; you've increased your status. But your work load has increased, which has forced you to work longer hours and bring work home. You've discovered that many of the meetings are extremely dull. And your boss has been critical of your performance at some of the meetings. If you provided for adequate monitoring in your plan, you'll detect these developing problems early and will be able to modify or reverse actions you've taken.

TAKING CHARGE of YOUR DIRECTION

Planning is not a panacea. Regardless of how carefully you try to anticipate problems and prepare for them, you can't gain complete control over your life and your career. Many unforeseen problems will develop. Many things are beyond your control; you can't prepare adequately for them but if you don't have a plan, you won't be able to influence your future. All you will be able to do is react to problems after they are fully developed, perhaps too late to do anything about them.

On the other hand, by planning, you can be self-initiating and make things happen. Of course, not everything will work out the way you want it to. But at least you will have done something positive to influence the future.

Everybody can benefit from life and career planning. But if you become nonpromotable, it's absolutely essential to work out a plan. On the down side of your career, you may become a victim of competence loss. You'll need a course of action to help you to maintain and develop your skills as well as keep your job.

Even if you manage to avoid losing competence, the fact that you have mastered your job will mean you'll have to battle against boredom and dissatisfaction. Planning can help you find ways to overcome these feelings by making your job more challenging.

Job dissatisfaction and boredom spill over into your home life, which can create tensions and psychosomatic illnesses. Planning can help you to better cope with these problems. It can also help you solve problems at home that spill over into your job.

Invest in your future! Start planning and influence the direction of your life and your career. Your time investment will be modest for the substantial returns planning can give you.

CHAPTER FOURTEEN

A Final Message

I haven't tried in this book to supply final answers to the problem of nonpromotability because I don't have any. It's a universal, persistent problem that, in my opinion, can be treated but not cured.

I believe I have helped focus attention on the problem by writing about it. Hopefully, some of the concepts I've presented will convince you that something positive can be done about it.

I have been successful if I have convinced you that both managers and subordinates must be willing to cooperate in order to establish favorable conditions to deal with the problem. The ideal relationship is one of interdependence as well as willingness to change attitudes and values.

A manager who wants to be a helper must be willing to invest time and company resources in doing something about preventing the progressively destructive effects of nonpromotability. He should initiate an ongoing dialog in which he demonstrates genuine concern with and interest in shared problem solving in establishing reciprocal trust and openness. By so doing he demonstrates that he has no intention of "putting subordinates on the shelf" and forgetting them. His primary objective should be to shift subordinate interests from the pursuit of personal advancement to self-improvement and achievement.

However, no matter how strong the desire of the manager to help a subordinate, he can't succeed without cooperating actively. He must not only be receptive to help; he must be fully aware of his need for it. He has to recognize what's happening to him, as well as the potential damage to his future career and to his life, as his work and life are interrelated. He must allow his manager and others to assist him. He does this by confiding in them and disclosing his feelings. He must be willing to initiate change in his life instead of resisting it. He must continue to learn and grow throughout his career. Instead of trying to maintain what he has, he must actively seek more from work and life — not more in terms of "bigger and better," but by doing things that will add to his personal satisfaction and feelings of self-worth.

Most importantly, the subordinate, or helpee, can take positive action to influence the direction of his future career rather than react to crises. By planning ahead and setting goals, he can gain greater confidence in himself and his future.

Perhaps the most significant advice I believe I can give anybody concerned about nonpromotability is: *You can minimize its negative effects if you choose to confront it and experiment with ways to deal with it.*

Index

adaptation
  job inventory and, 209–213
  rethinking values in, 213–218
  right feelings in, 204–209
Adult Learner, The (Knowles), 52
aggression, of "lifer" 194–195
aging careers
  case histories of, 123–127
  plan for, 123–127
  redirection of, 119–129
aging employee, capitalizing on, 127–129
appraisal, performance, *see* performance appraisal

boss, rating of, 150–153
boss-to-be, influence of, 154–155

career paths, mistakes in, 13–14
career planning, 220–238
  see also life/career planning
competitiveness, promotion and, 158–159
control, internal or external, 219
counseling, 23–41
  characteristics, self-evaluation in, 36–39
  common problems in, 27–31
  developed, 27, 31
  disciplinary, 26–30
  evaluative, 26–29
  failures in, 39–41
  formal, 25–27
  instructional, 26–28
  problem-solving, 27
counseling interview
  motivating environment and, 87
  worksheet, 31–36
counsellor, experienced vs. inexperienced, 34–36
current job, vs. new, 175

daily work record, 71-72
desensitization, in development process, 54–55
destructive mismatches, untangling of, 130–145
development, 42–60
  case histories in, 48–50, 52–54
  guided experience in, 52–55
  as investment or waste, 42–45
  methods of, 52–56
  modeling for, 55–56
  progressive desensitization in, 54–55
  in training, 45–48
  whole person in, 48–50
developmental interview, 56–60
distrust, promotability and, 160
"downhill blues," 122

early warning system, for nonpromotability, 17–21
education factor, 20
Edwards Personal Preference Schedule, 7

entangling alliances, 130–134
external control, vs. internal, 219

failing subordinate, salvaging of, 140–144
Fairleigh Dickinson University, 157, 191
fantasy
   job change as, 180–184
   of "lifer," 193
fear, 15–16
fixation stage
   of "lifer", 195–196
   in nonpromotability, 5–9, 119
French, John R. P., Jr., 100 n.

Gellerman, Saul, 80
General Electric Company, 100
goals and standards, agreement on, 110–115

helping appraisal process, 107–115
   advantages of, 116–117
higher-level position, promotion from, 160–163

internal control, vs. external, 219
interpersonal relationships, 20

job change, 168–184
   as escape, 170, 180–184
   internal, 178–180
   job evaluation and, 171–178
job dissatisfaction
   degrees of, 68–71
   potential for, 51
job enrichment, 66–72
job evaluation, job change and, 171–178
job inventory, 209–213
job mismatches, 130–131
job redesign, 73–78
job satisfaction, 51
   decline in, 189
   degrees of, 68–71
job staleness
   causes of, 65–66
   daily work record and, 71–72
   job enrichment in, 66–72
   motivation and, 66
   responsibility and, 65–66
   time and, 65

Kay, Emmanuel, 100 n.
Knowles, Malcolm, 52

life/career planning, 220–238
   action phase in, 235–237
   avoidance of, 220–224
   evaluating alternatives in, 235
   life and work objectives in, 229–235
   payoff in, 224–225
   "taking charge" in, 237–238
   worksheet in, 226
life/career target planning, 225–228
life objectives, 230–231
"lifer"
   coping with common reactions of, 198–201
   fixation of, 195–196
   positive energy of, 200
   rationalization of, 194
   recognition "blinders" of, 192–198
   regression of, 197–198
   work habits and attitudes of, 185–201
low energy, promotion and, 162
lower-level position, promotion from, 157–160

McGregor, Douglas,, 102–103
manager, mishandling of performance-appraisal interview by, 101
managerial development, see development
Maslow, Abraham H., 80
Meyer, Herbert H., 100 n.
Mike, Allen L., 7
mismatches, 130–145
   managerial, 131–133
   probable outcome of, 135–136
Mostel, Zero, 102
motivating environment, 79–97
   behavioral problems and, 79–80
   case histories, 88–89
   definition of, 80–81
   measurement of, 87–90
   strategies for creation of, 91
   subordinate–superior contribution to, 81–87
mutual distrust, promotion and, 160

negative behavior, strategies for attacking, 90–97
new job, vs. current, 175–176
nonpromotability
   see also nonpromotables; promotability; promotion

nonpromotability (*Continued*)
  adapting successfully to, 202–209
  appeal in, 166–167
  basic, 13
  boss's rating in, 150–153
  career path in, 13–14
  case histories in, 6–11
  certainty of, viii
  challenging verdict of, 163–167
  declining satisfaction and, 189
  decreased productivity and, 188–189
  early warning system in, 17–21
  education factor in, 20
  effects of, 188–192
  escape from, 180–184
  fear and other emotions in, 15–16
  fixation stage of, 5–9, 119, 195–196
  impact of, vii
  interpersonal relationships in, 163
  interview and, 155–156
  job change and, 168–184
  job inventory and, 209–213
  judges, criteria, and methods for, 150–157
  justness of, 164–166
  low energy and, 162
  no-win situations, 13
  onset of, 4–11
  politics of, 14–15
  poor work habits and, 162–163
  process of, 3–22
  recognition "blinders" in, 192–198
  real vs. perceived, 12–13
  rethinking of values, 213–220
  right feelings and, 204–209
  special tests for, 156–157
  stigma of, 3
  superior–subordinate relationships and, 23
  temperament changes in, 189–192
  temporary vs. permanent, 12
  third-party judges, 153–154
  understanding, 21–22
  voluntary vs. involuntary, 11–12
  whys and wherefores of, 11–17
  work history factor, 20
  yardstick for, 149–167
Nonpromotables
  counseling of, 23–41
  defined, v
  happy vs. unhappy, 50–52
  "lifer" as, 185–201
  motivating factor for, 186

older employee, assets of, 127–129
O'Neill, George, 214
O'Neill, Nena, 214

past conflicts, promotion and, 158
past performances, 16–17
peer comparison ratings, 169
performance appraisal, 98–118
  conventional, 103–105
  "helping," 106–117
  managerial rejection of conventional form of, 103–104
  manager's mishandling of, 101–102
  mishandling of, 100–103
performance contract, 110–115
performance goals and standards, agreement on, 110–115
personal growth, lack of, 161–162
planning, "taking charge" in, 237–238
  see also life/career planning
politics, effect of, 14–15
poor work habits, promotability and, 162–163
problem solving, counseling and, 30–31
productivity, decreased, 188–189
promotability, past performance and past mistakes in, 16–17
  see also nonpromotability
promotables
  defined, v
  motivating factors for, 186
  see also nonpromotables
promotion
  competition for, v
  importance of, 11
  from higher-level position, 160–163
  from lower-level position, 157–160
  poor communications and, 159

rationalization, of "lifer," 194
recognition "blinders," 192–198
regression, of "lifer," 197–198
right feelings, choice of, 204–209

self-esteem, of "lifer," 199
self-evaluation, of counseling characteristics, 36–39
senior employees, anger and anxiety of, 121–122
situational mismatches, 133–135

staleness, attitudes toward, 61–65
 see also job staleness
stale people
 awareness of, 62–64
 concern of, 62–64
 revitalizing of, 61–78
 unawareness of, 65
subordinate
 attention to, 44
 attitude change in, 139–140
 demotion or transfer of, 140
 job or situation restructuring for, 140
 motivation and, 82–87
 potential value of, 142
 progress report on, 143–144
 rehabilitation of, 139–144
 termination interview for, 144–145
 termination of, 136–138
 wandering, 79–80, 93
 warring, 80
 winding down, 90–92
 withdrawing type, 79–80, 92–93
 worrying, 96–97
subordinate–superior relationship, 23

temperament, changes in, 189–192
termination interview, 144–145
termination of subordinate
 alternatives to, 138–140
 cost of, 136–138
training, vs. development, 45–48

values, rethinking of, 213–218

"waiting" subordinate, 94
"wandering" subordinate, 79, 93–94
"warring" subordinate, 80, 95–96
What Are You Afraid Of? (Wood), 15–16
What Makes Sammy Run? 168
winding down behavior, 90–92
"withdrawing" subordinate, 79, 92–93
Wood, John T., 15–16
work history factor, 20
work objectives, 231–235
worrying subordinate, 96–97

younger employees, attitude of senior employees to, 122